ONE THING IS NEEDFUL WEEKLY DEVOTIONAL GUIDE

ONE THING IS NEEDFUL WEEKLY DEVOTIONAL GUIDE

52 doses of Scriptural insights to enrich your walk with God throughout the year

ANTHONY ADEFARAKAN

GLOEM, CANADA

Contents

WEEK ONE

WEEK TWO

WEEK THREE

WEEK FOUR

WEEK FIVE

WEEK SIX

WEEK SEVEN

WEEK EIGHT

WEEK NINE

WEEK TEN

WEEK ELEVEN

WEEK TWELVE

WEEK THIRTEEN

WEEK FOURTEEN

WEEK FIFTEEN

WEEK SIXTEEN

WEEK SEVENTEEN

WEEK EIGHTEEN

WEEK NINETEEN

WEEK TWENTY

WEEK TWENTY-ONE

WEEK TWENTY-TWO

WEEK TWENTY-THREE

WEEK TWENTY-FOUR

WEEK TWENTY-FIVE

WEEK TWENTY-SIX

WEEK TWENTY-SEVEN

WEEK TWENTY-EIGHT

WEEK TWENTY-NINE

WEEK THIRTY

WEEK THIRTY-ONE

WEEK THIRTY-TWO

WEEK THIRTY-THREE

WEEK THIRTY-FOUR

WEEK THIRTY-FIVE

WEEK THIRTY-SIX

WEEK THIRTY-SEVEN

WEEK THIRTY-EIGHT

WEEK THIRTY-NINE

WEEK FORTY

WEEK FORTY-ONE

WEEK FORTY-TWO

WEEK FORTY-THREE

WEEK FORTY-FOUR

WEEK FORTY-FIVE

WEEK FORTY-SIX

WEEK FORTY-SEVEN

WEEK FORTY-EIGHT

WEEK FORTY-NINE

WEEK FIFTY

WEEK FIFTY-ONE

WEEK FIFTY-TWO

BECOME A FINANCIAL PARTNER WITH JESUS

ABOUT THE AUTHOR

One Thing Is Needful
(One – TIN)
Weekly Devotional Guide
[52 doses of Scriptural insights to enrich your walk with God throughout the year]

Written by Anthony O. Adefarakan

WITH JESUS COMPLIMENTS

This devotional is produced by **Global Emancipation Ministries – Calgary** through the generosity of our Lord Jesus Christ. As a gift to the Body of Christ, permission is given to churches and religious organizations to freely copy excerpts from this material and make them available wherever there is need. Also, permission is given to missions organizations to translate this devotional to other languages for use on cross-cultural mission fields across the world. However, all copied excerpts and translations must acknowledge *"One Thing Is Needful (One-TIN) Devotional Guide"* as the source and also give the ministry's name.

OUR CONTACT

Global Emancipation Ministries - Calgary
Canada.
Phone: +1 587 9735910, +1 587 9695910
WhatsApp: +1 587 9735910
Email: info@gloem.org, emancipation4souls@yahoo.com
Facebook: https://www.facebook.com/gloem.org
Website: www.gloem.org

WHY YOU REALLY NEED JESUS!

You might have heard a lot of Preachers talk about the importance of surrendering one's life to Jesus and even the dangers of not doing so at one time or the other without you being really moved. But with these three (3) important reasons highlighted below, I strongly believe you will not need another sermon before deciding to yield to His saving grace regardless of your religious beliefs.

1. You have an Enemy to overcome
There is an adversary who is all out to steal from you, kill you and destroy you regardless of your level of education, moral uprightness, societal influence or even religious beliefs. He is Devil by name (John 10:10, 1 Peter 5: 8), and he doesn't release any of his captives until he completely destroys their souls in hell. The ONLY One Who can deliver you from his manipulations and also save your soul from him is Jesus Christ.

2. You have an Appointment to keep
Being alive and reading this implies you have a very important and inevitable appointment to keep. It is an appointment with death (Hebrews 9:27). Death is the sure end of all mortals (of which you are part); and to enable you prepare for this appointment without fear of eternal damnation, you need Jesus. He is the ONLY One Who has power over death (Revelation 1:18).

3. You have a Judge to face
Upon departure from this earth, you will have to stand before a judg-

ment throne to render an account of your earthly life (Hebrews 9:27, Romans 14:12). The outcome of this judgment is what will determine your eternal abode which will either be Heaven or the Lake of fire. Interestingly, the Judge Who will preside over your case and also decide where you will spend your eternity is Jesus (John 5:21-30, 2 Timothy 4:1). I perceive you are thinking "is God not our Judge? Why Jesus?" Well, you are not wrong. But God the Father Himself is the One Who handed over all the judgment to His Son, Jesus Christ. Read the verse 22 of that John chapter 5. So Jesus is the ONLY One Who has the power to either judge you guilty or guiltless in eternity.

Now that you know these, the wisest thing you can do for yourself is to quickly establish a relationship with Jesus, since you don't even know how close your appointment with death is. To do this, say this prayer aloud:

"Lord Jesus, I am a sinner and I cannot help myself. Wash me in your precious blood and make me a new creature. I open the door of my heart to you today, come into my life and become my Lord and Savior. Grant me the grace to overcome the devil, prepare me for eternity and help me to escape the judgment reserved for sinners. Thank You Jesus for saving me. Amen."

Congratulations! You are now SAVED. Go and sin no more.

To learn more about your new relationship with Jesus, kindly send an Email to info@gloem.org or emancipation4souls@yahoo.com, we will send you a material that will help you. You can also call, text or whatsapp +1 587 9735910 or +1 587 9695910 for further assistance.

Dearly Beloved,
Life on earth has been described as a form of pilgrimage (1 Peter 2:11, Hebrews 11:13) with eternity as man's final destination.

In the course of this brief earthly sojourn, we are bound to face certain situations capable of generating questions like *'what step do I take?' 'where do I settle?' 'who do I marry?' 'will I be rich or poor?' 'how do I finance my projects?' 'how do I take good care of my family?' 'how do I know God's will for my life?'* just to mention a few. Usually, we find it difficult to provide correct answers to these questions due to our weak mortal nature.

However, there is a manual for this pilgrimage, which is the Word of God. The One Who designed this journey for us has put in the manual all we need to navigate our way successfully and to eventually end up on the glorious side of eternity when the pilgrimage is over. Little wonder David prayed in Psalm 119:19 – *"I am a stranger in the earth; hide not thy commandment from me".*

In this **One Thing Is Needful (One – TIN) Weekly Devotional Guide**, the Lord will be opening our eyes to divine insights from His Word, capable of enriching our walk with Him throughout the year as well as providing answers to the questions on our minds and pointing us in the right path to take in order to experience a fulfilled life here on earth and to attain a glorious eternity when the journey is over.

This is not written like the daily devotionals we are already used to which we sometimes read in the morning before going out but by the time we are back in the evening can hardly remember what we read earlier in the day. It is a weekly devotional guide because it will encourage us to spend a whole week prayerfully pondering the divine revelation caught in the course of our study until it sinks deep into our spirits and we naturally begin to daily walk in it. Jesus Christ commended Mary's choice of spending time listening to His Words according to Luke 10:39, and thereafter declared her choice as the '**one thing that is needful**'. It is my prayer that as we give the Word of God the first place in our hearts every time and continually meditate on it as we daily go about our activities, His light and glory will overshadow us and all our endeavors in Jesus' Name.

As you encounter the secret things the Lord has revealed by His Spirit in this guide, determine to prayerfully apply them in your life and situations; you will record unusual testimonies and God's light will shine upon your ways – Job 22:28, Psalm 119:105.

Also, remember to share these insights with your family and friends. It's a major way of spreading the light of God into every dark area of their lives.

Be blessed as you read on.

Anthony O. Adefarakan
President, Global Emancipation Ministries – Calgary

Week One

Study Focus: Why Certain Prophecies Are Not Fulfilled
Scriptural Text: I Samuel 10:9

<u>Insights for Meditation and Prayerful Application</u>
Numbers 23:19 says *"God is not a man, that He should lie, neither the son of man, that He should repent: hath He said, and shall He not do it? Or hath He spoken, and shall He not make it good?"*
Prophecies are true statements or declarations from God; and if He were not willing to fulfill them, He would not give them as prophecies in the first place. But true as these prophecies are, it is important to note that you will have to pray them into manifestation as none of them will just fall on your laps. Also, you should know by now that the devil seeks to oppose every plan of God for man, so prayers will have to be offered to combat and frustrate the plans of the devil against the fulfillment of God's counsel towards you - *(1 Timothy 1:18, 2 Corinthians 10:3-6)*. However, while prayers are being offered, there are two other main requisites for these prophecies to find eventual fulfillment in any man's life. They are:

1. A New Heart (or a new attitude), and
2. An Open Gate.

Let's consider these conditions in a more detailed form.
1. **A New Heart (or a new attitude).**
1 Samuel 10:9 says *"And it was so, that when he had turned his back to go from Samuel, God gave him **another heart**, and all these signs came to pass that day."* The Living Bible Translation (TLB) says "...*God gave him a*

***new attitude**, and all of Samuel's prophecies came true that day"*. [Emphasis mine].

The implication of this is that God has a lot of prophecies documented for His children in the Bible, and He might even have spoken certain things to you directly or through His Prophets – all of which are true statements from Him. But to see them come to pass in your own life, you need to possess the right kind of heart (attitude). Your state of heart at the point of receiving the prophecy may not be capable of delivering the fulfillment. Prophecies are not things that have happened, neither are they things happening, rather they are things that will happen. Therefore, your attitude must change in order to align with the things God is about to do. Until your heart or attitude changes, you may remain in your present state –carrying all the prophecies about in your diary without seeing any of them being fulfilled. Can you now see we are the ones preventing the fulfillment of our prophecies most of the time? To experience the fulfillment of all the mouth of the Lord has spoken concerning you, you will have to deliberately offer yourself to the Lord for a change of heart (attitude). Remember, the fulfillment of a prophecy is not just a function of the validity of the Source but of the solidity of the faith of the recipient demonstrated through taking appropriate steps towards its fulfillment.

For instance, the Lord has promised a man a whale (a big fish that lives in large seas) through a prophetic declaration and he claimed it. Then, in order to get the prophecy fulfilled, the man takes his "hook and line" and goes to a flowing stream near his house to fish for the whale. Will such an action ever fetch that man the promised whale? It's not possible, because you can't get whales in flowing streams; the best you can get are Tilapias (small fish). If the man really wanted to possess the right attitude for the fulfillment of that promise, he would get a massive trawler (not hook and line) and go to the big seas where whales are, engaging the services of expert whale catchers because just an individual cannot successfully capture a whale. Just by taking these actions, the man has literally positioned himself for obtaining the whale God promised him. No matter how much you fast and pray, you will never get a whale in a stream. If you want whales, you have to go to where whales are.

Also, a barren woman who has received a prophecy of fruitfulness is expected to stop entertaining pity, sorrow and sympathy over her situation; but should rather start thinking like a mother by getting baby materials, listening to talks through CDs and tapes on how to be a successful mother, reading books on joyful parenting among other things needed for mothers. That's the kind of attitude that can deliver the fulfillment of the prophecy to her, not an attitude of pity or barrenness. This was how Hannah got her own baby in 1 Samuel 1: 17-18. Your attitude must change before you can experience a change.

2. **An Open Gate.**

Isaiah 60:11 says *"Therefore your gates shall be open continually, they shall not be shut day or night that men may bring to you the wealth of Gentiles, and their kings in procession."*

This implies that for your prophecies to be fulfilled, you will have to stay open and be receptive to their manifestations. The tenth verse of this chapter according to The Living Bible Translation (TLB) says *"Foreigners will come and build your cities, presidents and kings will send you aid..."* God really meant this, together with His other promises in this chapter 60 of the Book of Isaiah; but to experience them you've got to keep your gates opened at all times (round the clock). This is very important because when the Lord brings the wealth of the Gentiles to you as He promised and meets your gates shut, He would be helpless in delivering them to you. In 2Kings 3: 16-20, the Lord spoke through Elisha that the valley shall be filled with water but the people needed to dig trenches so as to receive the promised water. If the water had come as prophesied without the trenches available to retain it, it would not have stayed; it would have disappeared through evaporation. Thus, in order to receive their water (as spoken by the Lord), they had to **open their gates** by digging trenches to receive the water in.

In this information age, you can ensure your gates are continually open by keeping your communication lines open – let your phone always be available to receive calls and SMS capable of transforming your destiny. Ensure you are reachable; let your battery not go flat before you recharge it. Ensure your line is always available, you never can tell which call will birth your miracles.

Also, keep your information channels open – let your mind be open to information through TVs, Radio, internet, newspapers, magazines, friends etc. Train your mind, eyes, and ears to be open to new information. Don't despise any idea, give it a thought. Be ready to receive your promise through whichever way God chooses to bring it to you. Ask questions, make enquiries and be on the alert for the 'wealth of the Gentiles' coming. That is how to get prophecies fulfilled in your life, not by just sitting down claiming their manifestations.

Note: Keep meditating on these insights throughout this week and prayerfully apply them to relevant areas of your life and even those of others.

Prayer Focus: Say these prayers for each day as you meditate on the insights received.

Day 1: Father, thank You for all Your beautiful promises and prophecies over my life.

Day 2: Father, please deliver me from delayed manifestation of your promises.

Day 3: Father, please create in me the right heart and attitude. Let there be manifestation.

Day 4: Father, I open the gates of my life to Your favor. Send help to me speedily.

Day 5: Father, cause me to be remembered for good. Let my helpers locate me speedily.

Day 6: Father, please take away every reproach in my life. Liberate me by Your mercy.

Day 7: Father, I will praise You all the days of my life. Fill my mouth with testimonies.

Week Two

Study Focus: God Has a Plan for Your Life
Scriptural Text: Genesis 2:15-23

<u>Insights for Meditation and Prayerful Application</u>
"The Lord God placed the man in the Garden of Eden as its gardener, to tend and care for it..." Genesis 2:15-23 (TLB).
Before God created man, He first created the world he would live in. Before He placed man in Eden, He already planted the garden with various trees and supplied it with rivers. All the man had to do was just to tend and care for it; that was his purpose for being in Eden. God thereafter gave him a clear instruction for living which he was expected to strictly adhere to. (Verses16-17).In addition to this, God gave him an appointment he never applied for and a wife he didn't ask for. (Verses 18-23).

How does this relate to you?
As a person living on this earth, your purpose was established long before you were born. (Jeremiah 1:4-5). Your reason for living is well known to God, and He is eager to reveal it to you. God will never place you in an 'Eden' just to be looking; He surely has a plan for you there. For Adam, He was to tend and care for it; so you are also on earth to do something. Get saved – be born again - and thereafter ask in prayer; find out from God, He will show you your own assignment. He will tell you what to 'tend and care for'. Once your purpose is established by reason of your discovery; appointments, opportunities etc you did not even pray for will start locating you. Also, you won't have to necessarily pray for a spouse as a youth; God will naturally connect you to your

mate. In your purpose lies all you will ever need to be fulfilled in life; outside this, struggling is inevitable.

However, God also gave Adam a 'warning for living'; and this is true of you as well. In fulfilling your purpose, there are things you must not do and there are things you may do. One thing you must not be found doing as a purpose – conscious person is SINNING. This can cost you your fulfillment in life.

So, be born of God, discover your purpose, start working and walking in line with your purpose, obey all the warnings you are given by your Maker (as contained in the Bible), and all you will ever need to be fulfilled in life will be made available to you. You won't have to pray at times before your needs are met. May your life here on earth cooperate with God's plan for you. Amen.

Note: Keep meditating on these insights throughout this week and prayerfully apply them to relevant areas of your life and even those of others.

Prayer Focus: Say these prayers for each day as you meditate on the insights received.

Day 1: Father, thank You for creating me in Your precious image and likeness.

Day 2: Father please in any ways I have been displeasing You, kindly forgive me.

Day 3: Father, I want to live in line with Your purpose. Please reveal it to me.

Day 4: Father, take away every veil preventing me from knowing You intimately.

Day 5: Father, please keep me at the very center of Your will and purpose for my life.

Day 6: Father, all I need to fulfill my destiny in You, please supply them speedily.

Day 7: Father, let all Your plans for my life begin to manifest without further delays.

Week Three

Study Focus: What Gratitude Does To Your Faith Life
Scriptural Text: Romans 4:20-21

<u>**Insights for Meditation and Prayerful Application**</u>
Isaiah 51:2 (AKJV) says *"Look unto Abraham your father...I called him alone, and blessed him, and increased him"*.
The Christian journey is that of faith in the reality of the unseen rather than the things which are seen. In God's family, 'seeing is not believing' rather it is 'believing is seeing'. You don't see until you believe, because it is what you believe that determines what you see.
Faith is not just a virtue, but also an essential requirement if one must please God and walk with Him (Heb.11:6). Abraham, our father of faith, was called by God into a journey to an unknown but sure destination. The Bible says *'...he went out, not knowing whither he went'* (Heb. 11:8b). One character in the scriptures who exhibited an unwavering faith in God was Abraham, and He got what God promised him.
How did he receive his promised blessing? **He showed gratitude to the One who gave him the promise while awaiting its fulfillment.** Romans 4:20-21 says *'He staggered not at the promise of God through unbelief; but was strong in faith, **giving glory to God**; and being fully persuaded, that what He had promised, He was able also to perform'*.
Many a journey of faith has terminated in defeat and depression due to the absence of this ingredient called gratitude. The God Who made the promise is not a man who says a thing today and says another thing tomorrow (Num 23:19). He honors His word more than His Name (Psalm 138:2) and He remains unchanged throughout eternity (Malachi 3:6). If you claim to be exercising the Biblical faith and you are not giving

thanks and glory to God for what you are expecting Him to do, then your faith stands the risk of being shipwrecked. However, if you will learn from Abraham our father who gave thanks to God for the birth of Isaac (the promised child) even before he was born, your faith will always deliver expected results regardless of the magnitude of the promise or the period of waiting. Give glory to God for your expectations, then and only then will you become qualified to experience their physical manifestation. On the other hand, complaining, grumbling and murmuring will not only further delay their manifestations but also bring you under God's judgment (Num 14:26-30). Practice gratitude, it wins every time!

Note: Keep meditating on these insights throughout this week and prayerfully apply them to relevant areas of your life and even those of others.

Prayer Focus: Say these prayers for each day as you meditate on the insights received.

Day 1: Father, I thank You for everything You have done in my life till now.

Day 2: Father, I thank You for every promise You have fulfilled in my life.

Day 3: Father, I thank You for Your integrity. You always fulfill Your promises.

Day 4: Father, I give You glory for the manifestation of my expectations.

Day 5: Father, I praise You because I know You will never fail me.

Day 6: Father, please help my faith. Deliver me from doubts and unbelief.

Day 7: Father, help me to live a victorious life here on earth. Solve all my problems.

Week Four

Study Focus: Litmus Test for Your Pastor
Scriptural Text: Jeremiah 3:15

Insights for Meditation and Prayerful Application

In Jeremiah 3:15, the Almighty God said "...*I will give you pastors according to mine heart, which shall feed you with knowledge and understanding*".

From this scripture, it means there are some pastors after God's heart; and they are easily recognized by their ability and willingness to feed the flock (church of God) with knowledge and understanding. That is their primary assignment.

Now that you know the mandate given to your pastors, are they really fulfilling it?

Here is a litmus test for your pastor: If your Pastor keeps preaching and preaching with your notes full of sermon topics but does not ensure your knowledge and understanding of the Word and ways of God, that scripture is not being fulfilled in his/her life.

Ask yourself, 'is my Pastor really feeding me with knowledge and understanding?' If the answer is yes, please keep listening to him/her; but if the answer is no, kindly locate 'a Pastor after God's heart who shall feed you with knowledge and understanding'.

Why? It is what you know that determines what answers to you and what doesn't in this life and in the one to come.

May the Lord grant you the wisdom to choose rightly!

Note: Keep meditating on these insights throughout this week and prayerfully apply them to relevant areas of your life and even those of others.

Prayer Focus: Say these prayers for each day as you meditate on the insights received.

Day 1: Father, thank You for giving the Body of Christ Pastors after Your own heart.

Day 2: Father, please increase the knowledge and wisdom of all our Pastors.

Day 3: Father, please expose and deal with every unrepentant false teacher.

Day 4: Father, please urgently deliver Your children from wolves in sheep skins.

Day 5: Father, shield all Your Pastors from arrows of wickedness. Protect their families.

Day 6: Father, help my Pastor to fulfill Your call upon his life.

Day 7: Father, use me to be a blessing to my Pastor.

Week Five

Study Focus: Journey Back To Innocence
Scriptural Text: Genesis 2:16-17

<u>Insights for Meditation and Prayerful Application</u>
"But the Lord God gave the man this warning: 'You may eat any fruit in the garden, except fruit from the Tree of Conscience-for its fruit will open your eyes to make you aware of right and wrong, good and bad. If you eat its fruit, you will be doomed to die.'"- Genesis 2:16-17(TLB).
God's original plan for man was '**innocence**' and not '**conscience**'. There was no plan that man would ever be judged because you don't judge an innocent person. The state of Adam and Eve before the fall was that of a little baby – who is not conscious of its nakedness, foes, friends, animals, danger, pride etc -just innocent. If taken to a zoo (where animals are kept), and the gate to a lion's cage were opened, a little baby will literally crawl in to touch the lion without any fear of attack. That's why Moses could be put at a river's edge without him screaming, he was a baby- 3months old. (Exodus 2:3). That's also the reason a naked Adam could name all the animals including the ones now known as wild animals without any fear; they were mere pets in his hands.
But after the fall, the conscience of man came alive. And unfortunately, due to the weak human nature, man often tends towards doing evil than doing right- being a sinful being by nature. Because of disobedience innocence gave way to conscience and as a result, judgment must take place to reward either the good or bad done. For instance when a child is born, it is born an innocent being (God's initial plan); but because sin lies in its human nature, as he begins to grow the sinful nature starts manifesting (by reason of conscience). With time, this child begins to

find it difficult to overcome his sinful desires- this is the fallen state of man. (Romans 7:15-24). But thanks be to God; **WITH THE SACRIFICE OF JESUS CHRIST, MAN CAN BE MADE RIGHT WITH GOD AGAIN.** Although the conscience is still there, the power to overcome sin and choose good has been given through Jesus Christ. So, when a man accepts the Lordship of Christ over his life, he is given the grace to have his conscience purified, then the ability to say 'no' to evil and 'yes' to good is imparted to him. (Hebrews10:22).

Thus, at the judgment, he will be vindicated just as one who was originally innocent. I mean, the same way an innocent man would not be condemned; a saved sinner (though still with conscience) will not be condemned because of the power at work in him which has made him choose good against evil. Romans 8:1-2 says no condemnation awaits those who belong to Jesus Christ.

Therefore to be free as Adam was before the fall, you need JESUS. Without this, you are lost forever regardless of how good you may feel now- John 3:18-19. And it is only then the devil will be free to rejoice over you in hell. You must receive Jesus Christ before you leave this earth; that is the only way you would not be condemned on the LAST DAY when He shall come to judge the whole world. Revelation 22:12. **Decide for Jesus NOW!!!**

Note: Keep meditating on these insights throughout this week and prayerfully apply them to relevant areas of your life and even those of others.

Prayer Focus: Say these prayers for each day as you meditate on the insights received.

Day 1: Father, thank You for the sacrifice of Your dear Son Jesus Christ for all sinners.

Day 2: Lord Jesus, please sprinkle my conscience with Your precious Blood.

Day 3: Lord Jesus, please empower me to choose right desires over evil ones.

Day 4: Father, destroy every form of carnality in me. Purify my heart.

Day 5: Father, release upon me the grace to live holy. Let sin not have dominion over me.

Day 6: Father, let sinners all over the world come to the knowledge of Your saving grace.

Day 7: Father, please preserve me blameless till I see Your face in glory.

Week Six

Study Focus: The Final Battle
Scriptural Text: Hebrews 9:27

Insights for Meditation and Prayerful Application
On the 14th day of September 1998, I had the opportunity of watching someone die in my very presence for the first time. It was my grandmother's demise, having lived with us for about five years.

While Mama was alive she played with us (the grandchildren), told us local stories, taught us local songs, told us funny things about ourselves while we were still babies among other interesting things. As a matter of fact, she took special interest in me just because she felt I'm like her husband whose demise occurred before I was born – she loved me so much and gave me more gifts than my other siblings. She always wanted me around her, and to achieve that she would often want me to do one thing or the other for her while others were playing. She literally engaged all the methods at her disposal to show me genuine love.

But a night came, after a brief sickness which had kept Mama indoors for a while; we were in the living room watching a movie when suddenly she called for something to be done for her in her room. I entered the room; and what I saw? Mama was already gasping i.e. her breath was ceasing. Frightened, I called my parents to come and look at her. By the time they arrived her breath was almost gone, with her eyeballs turning leaving only the white part. At that point my mum began to cry; and while I watched, I saw Mama struggling with death on her bed. She jerked, gasped, shed tears and even passed out urine in her battle with death. Eventually, the final result of the battle came – Mama gave up the ghost and was covered. Why did this happen? Well, it is written, *"And as it is appointed unto men once to die, but after this the judgment."(Heb 9:27)*. We were all there, but we couldn't help her in that battle; even I, Mama's lover boy, couldn't render any help at that instance because she was faced with **THE FINAL BATTLE** –which no one helps another to fight.

My dear friend, this story is that of Mama; but did you know it will soon be your turn? Certainly, it will. Thank God Mama died as a Christian; but when the time to face your own final battle comes –when your spouse, children, uncle, aunt, tradition, chieftaincy titles, sacrifices, secret societies, cult members, juju priest or even your Pastor/Reverend will be unable to help you, are you sure JESUS –The Lover of your soul – will be there to receive your soul into eternity in Paradise? If No is your sincere answer, then you have automatically subscribed to eternal shame and condemnation without even knowing it. However, there is a way out; quickly accept the Lordship of Jesus Christ over your life now. You can do this by saying this short prayer: **_Dear Lord Jesus, I am a sinner. Please forgive me of all my sins. I accept you into my life today as my personal Lord and Saviour. Help me to live a holy life beginning from now. Thank you for saving me._**

If you said that prayer, I congratulate you because you are now born again and Jesus Christ is now living in your heart. Ensure you find a Bible believing church and start worshipping there so as to know how to live this new life in Christ. You may tell the Pastor there about your new birth and he will help you know more about running this race. **Please stay pure and abstain from sin; the FINAL BATTLE MAY BE NEARER THAN YOU THINK!**

Note: Keep meditating on these insights throughout this week and prayerfully apply them to relevant areas of your life and even those of others.

Prayer Focus: Say these prayers for each day as you meditate on the insights received.
Day 1: Father, thank You for being a Man of war.

Day 2: Father, I praise You for all the battles You have been fighting for me.

Day 3: Father, please let me see You before I see death.

Day 4: Father, preserve my spirit, soul and body blameless till I see You in glory.

Day 5: Father, please destroy the yoke of untimely death in my family.

Day 6: Father, please let Your judgment be in my favour in eternity.

Day 7: Father, I receive Your gift of long life for me and my family members.

Week Seven

Study Focus: Now in Christ? You Need To Know These
Scriptural Text: John 1:12

<u>**Insights for Meditation and Prayerful Application**</u>
"But to all who did receive him, who believed in his name, he gave the right to become children of God" – John 1: 12 ESV
We really want to congratulate you on your wise decision to accept Jesus Christ as your Lord and Saviour.
As a result of this decision you have made, there is a celebration going on in heaven; the angels are rejoicing before God on your behalf.
"...there is joy in the presence of the angels of God over one sinner that repenteth" –Luke 15:10.
Now that you have become a child of God, there are five (5) important things you need to know and do in order to remain in God's family.

1. Read, Study and Meditate on the Word of God Every day
1 Peter 2:2 says *"As newborn babes, desire the sincere milk of the word, that ye may grow thereby"*.
You must realize that you now have a new life which you have never lived before. It is therefore important that you get into the Word of God - the Bible- to find out how you are expected to live and behave in God's family. This you can do by reading the Bible, memorizing its verses, studying it and meditating on its truths in order to become sanctified and spiritually mature. If you must grow and live a victorious Christian life designed for you on earth without going back to your old sinful ways, you need to live by the word of God – Matthew 4:4, Psalm 119:9,11.
To make this easier for you, you can start by studying the Gospel ac-

cording to St. John. You can read one chapter a day, and you will notice your appetite for God's word increasing.

2. Pray Everyday
1 Thessalonians 5:17 says *"Pray without ceasing".*
In this family, the language with which all God's children communicate with Him is prayer. You will have to learn to pray in order to communicate with your Father in heaven.
It is not a difficult task though; prayer simply means talking to God in the Name of Jesus. God wants to hear your voice in prayer, and He is willing to answer your prayers as well – Jeremiah 33:3a.
Don't bother yourself about being able to speak the right grammar; God knows your heart already. All He wants is your ability to use your mouth to tell Him what is in your heart in the language you can best express yourself with, and He will answer you because He understands all languages. Don't allow a day to pass without you talking to God – by thanking Him, praising Him for His good works and asking Him for whatever you need. Remember, He is now your Father.
Also in your prayers, ask Him for the baptism of the Holy Spirit. The Holy Spirit is your Helper Who will assist you to pray the right kind of prayers according to Romans 8: 26. If you ask, God will give you because He already promised to do so in Luke 11:13.

3. Fellowship Regularly with other Believers
Hebrews 10:25a (TM) says *"Not avoiding worshiping together as some do..."*
God has ordained the gathering together of His children from time to time, mainly for the purpose of fellowship and edification.
You will have to carefully and prayerfully locate a church around you where Jesus Christ is being honoured as the Lord and Saviour of mankind. Join the assembly and fellowship with the believers there. You can meet the Pastor in charge of such assembly and tell him/her you are a new member of God's family. Such a Pastor will offer you the necessary assistance you require to become established in the kingdom.
However, be very careful. Don't fall victim of false prophets running false churches. Make sure you pray and allow God to lead you to the right assembly.

4. Be actively engaged in Kingdom Service

John 9:4 says *"I must work the works of him that sent me, while it is day: the night cometh, when no man can work".*

God expects you to work for Him with the new life He has given you. As a matter of fact, *'you were saved to serve'*. Also, He rewards everyone who works for Him here on earth and even in eternity (Revelation 22:12).

Therefore, get engaged in kingdom services like singing in the choir, ushering in the church, visiting and following up new converts, cleaning of the sanctuary, organizing crusades, planting of churches, writing and printing of gospel tracts, sending of welfare materials to mission fields among others. None of these services will go unrewarded –Hebrews 6:10.

God has deposited some gifts and talents in you. Think about them; and once discovered, start using them to the glory of His Holy Name. That is what it means to engage in Kingdom service.

5. Become His Witness

Mark 16:15 says *"...Go ye into all the world, and preach the gospel to every creature".*

Someone told you about the love God has for sinners; you embraced it and you became born again – a child of God. Now that you know, it is your duty to tell others so that they too can be saved.

Use every opportunity you have to preach the gospel of Jesus Christ – through direct contact with persons, through sharing of tracts, Radio/TV broadcasts or any other relevant means.

God wants His family to increase in number, and He is depending on you to achieve this. That is why He saved your soul. Become His witness today; let others know that *JESUS STILL SAVES!*

Note: Keep meditating on these insights throughout this week and prayerfully apply them to relevant areas of your life and even those of others.

Prayer Focus: Say these prayers for each day as you meditate on the insights received.

Day 1: Father, thank You for redeeming my soul from eternal destruction.

Day 2: Father, please give me a strong appetite for meditating in Your Word.

Day 3: Father, please grant me the grace for an effective prayer life.

Day 4: Father, please surround my life with the right relationships.

Day 5: Father, please grant me the grace to be a useful vessel in Your Kingdom.

Day 6: Father, please empower me with the grace to tell others about You.

Day 7: Father, don't let me ever lose my salvation. Please uphold me to the end.

Week Eight

Study Focus: Ten "Don'ts" To Fulfilling Your Destiny
Scriptural Text: Hosea 4:6

Insights for Meditation and Prayerful Application
One of the greatest mistakes people make in life is that they engage in the things and activities that don't make them fulfill their God-ordained destiny. Consider the following and adhere to them if you really want your destiny fulfilled:

1. DON'T EVER WASTE YOUR TIME
God gave you time for all you have to do and you are responsible to maximize your time and your life to do all you have to do for God! You CAN'T DO EVERYTHING! You CAN'T GO EVERYWHERE!!
Your life is packaged in capsules of time. Who you spend your time with and how you spend your time is actually taking your life. Anyone who wastes your time is wasting your life.
You only have enough time for the MAIN ASSIGNMENT God sent you here to accomplish for Him. When time is no longer on your side at old age, make sure you have done the major things God sent you to do! Joshua at old age is a picture of the danger of wasting time on divine assignment **(Joshua 13:1-3).**

2. DON'T OVERLOOK SMALL PEOPLE WITH CRITICAL TOOLS FOR YOUR ASSIGNMENT
Most times in life and ministry, God will keep some of your greatest resources for the assignment in the lives and hands of the most unlikely people! Train your spirit and eyes to recognize small people with BIG tools for the assignment. For example;

1. The lad with the FIVE LOAVES **(John 6:9-10)**.
2. The house girl with the CRITICAL INFORMATION for Naaman **(2Kings 5:1-5)**.
3. The men of David **(1Samuel 22:1-2)**.

I have learnt that in any generation, the bulk of God's work is carried out by small people with critical tools who will give glory to God for the privilege of serving Him. It is easier for widows to give their MITES than for multimillionaires to give their life savings for God's work! If you are only looking for and at 'BIG PEOPLE' alone to get the work of God done you will be delayed and may not even be able to finish the work!

3. DON'T EVER WORRY ABOUT WHAT YOU CANNOT DO ANYTHING ABOUT

You will find out sooner than later in life and ministry that there are some matters you CANNOT do anything about! There are also some matters you are NOT SUPPOSED to do anything about in life and ministry! Always find your responsibility and bother about that, not any other thing! God handles things that you cannot do anything about. For example as a preacher, my responsibility is to get the message and preach it to the best of my ability. Whether people come or not or whether they listen or not is not my responsibility!

4. DON'T EVER VIOLATE PROCESS

The God of our destiny is a God of process. Don't ever violate the process of God in your life. The process is what determines the quality of the product! Don't try to get by prophecy what can only come through a process **(Rom 4:16-22)**. Your manifestation in life is a function of the process you have gone through under God.

5. DON'T MAKE PEOPLE EQUAL IN YOUR LIFE

Recognize that people are not the same in their contributions to your life. Reward people according to their contributions in your life. Never reward people equally in your life. Never reward them more or less than their contributions in your life. When you violate this major law of life, you will kill critical relationships in your life.

6. DON'T REACT AGAINST RIGHTEOUS CORRECTIONS
Psalm 141:5 "Let the righteous smite me; it shall be a kindness: and let him reprove me; it shall be an excellent oil, which shall not break my head"...
When you receive direction, correction must follow. The directions of wisdom call for human correction before profit can result. Excellence is the product of corrections from righteous sources in your life.

7. DON'T TOUCH WHATEVER GOD HAS FORBIDDEN FOR YOU
Recognize that on the road of destiny, there will be things that God will place a ban on for you. Whether He allows others to do it or not does not concern you. DON'T touch whatever God has forbidden for you; whether it is a person, a place, a thing, an attitude or an action.
Adam and Eve missed it here, Samson missed it with Delilah, David missed it with Bathsheba and Demas missed it with the world.
Gehazi received leprosy because he touched what his master rejected! Did you know that your marriage vow makes another person a banned item to you for sexual relations? Joseph recognized this and he fulfilled his calling.
The glory of God is not yours so don't touch it! Do a research on the things God has forbidden you to touch generally in the Bible, and then find out also what He has forbidden you SPECIFICALLY in your life through the Holy Spirit.

8. DON'T CARRY ON A CONVERSATION WITH THE DEVIL
Eve carried on a discussion with the devil and regretted forever; **Gen. 3:1-6** (pls. read). Jesus, our Lord refused to carry on a discussion with the devil and the human race is blessed for it forever. See **Matt. 4:3-11**. How does the devil converse with man? Through the mind basically; he talks to and with people through *thoughts, suggestions, imaginations*, etc. see **2Cor. 10:3-5**.
Whenever you find thoughts or reasoning going on in your mind that

are contrary to the word of God, you are in a conversation with the devil. If you don't stop the conversation, you will get into serious trouble. No one engages Satan in a discussion and goes unscathed! What should we do when Satan tries to engage us in a conversation?

1. Don't speak your own opinion. Rather, quote the word of God to him on the matter.
2. Rebuke him.
3. Bind the spirit he's using against you.
4. Remind him of his future doom from the Bible.

9. DON'T EVER LET SATAN MAKE THE THINGS OF GOD LOOK FOOLISH TO YOU

This is the biggest attack of Satan against a child of God or a minister as he tries to fulfill his destiny or discharge his duty in the ministry of the word and in the execution of his obedience to the voice of God. Satan can't stop the word of God, but if he can make a divine instruction you have received look foolish, he will stop you from carrying out that instruction. Once you do this, you disqualify yourself from receiving what the word of God promised. Many people have missed the best of God, including salvation and heaven on this single point: SATAN MADE THE PLAN OF GOD TO SOLVE THEIR PROBLEMS LOOK FOOLISH TO THEM.

Naaman would have died a leper if he did not break the attack of the devil in this area (**II Kings 5:1-15**). For a minister of the gospel, it is the stumbling block to the miraculous. What if you were Moses in front of the Red Sea? How reasonable did it sound to point a rod over a sea? What if you were Joshua before the wall of Jericho? How wise and strategic was it to make sound or shout and announce your presence in such obvious manner to your enemy? What if you were the servants who poured water into the pots and were told to draw it out as wine to the governor? Was that reasonable? The adviser to the king in **II Kings 6** who asked how a miracle would take place acted normally in a supernatural environment. You are foolish when you act normally in supernatural moments. This is because Satan must be making the things of God look foolish to you. **II Kings 6:24, 7:1-2, 16-20** (please read).

Remember being foolish and looking foolish are not the same! Most of the wisdom of God is hidden in things that 'look foolish' to a natural man! If it is God, it is wisdom; His wisdom is so high that a natural man cannot understand it. **1 Corinthians 2:14, 3:18-20. If it looks foolish to you, you will stumble at it. How do we conquer this attack? Become a fool to become wise.**

10. DON'T TRY TO FULFILL THE DIVINE COMMISSION WITH A SATANIC METHOD

The truth is that there is no right way to do a wrong thing, but there are many wrong ways to do a right thing. This is where the strategy of Satan is! He will offer you as a child of God a lot of alternatives to do the will of God in the wrong way.

Examples:

1. Jesus came to take back the kingdom of this world from the devil through the road of the cross. Satan offered it to Him by asking Him to bow to him! If this was done, the purpose of the cross would have been defeated. Each time you take the alternative offer the devil is presenting to you; you allow the purpose of God to be defeated in your own life.
2. God opens a door for a preacher to preach overseas and then he goes to bribe someone to get a visa to travel. If God opens a door for you to preach overseas, He will also ensure you get the visa.
3. A couple waiting on God for the fruit of the womb; the devil offers them adultery as an option. Anything that is an alternative to the way and the will of God must be from the devil.

Paul said in **Rom. 3:7**, "If God is glorified through my life, why then am I still judged a sinner?" People can glorify God in your life and God is judging you as a sinner. You can be doing the work of God and people are getting blessed but God is not happy with you. Satan knows that you can do the will of God in a wrong spirit so he will offer you that road and many times, it will be easier and cheaper than the right road but there will be no reward. What Satan will not tell anyone is that when you do the will of God with a satanic method or spirit; you will get Satan's judgment. What a tragedy!

If you want to do the will of God, see what the Lord says in **Matt. 7:21-23** and do it according to His will. Jesus said, *not everyone that calls Him Lord, Lord, will enter into the kingdom of heaven,* He said many will come and say in His name they did many mighty works but He will answer *I NEVER* knew you. The same will be for everyone who does the will of God in another way.

Note: Keep meditating on these insights throughout this week and prayerfully apply them to relevant areas of your life and even those of others.

Prayer Focus: Say these prayers for each day as you meditate on the insights received.

Day 1: Father, separate every time waster from my life.

Day 2: Father, deliver me from the schemes of the devil.

Day 3: Father, please don't let me ever miss my divinely ordained helpers.

Day 4: Father, I receive grace to never touch anything unclean and ungodly again.

Day 5: Father, please give me Your wisdom liberally and lavishly.

Day 6: Father, please create in me the right heart for my destiny fulfillment.

Day 7: Father, please help me to end my journey at Your right hand in eternity.

Week Nine

Study Focus: Top Secret: Death Has a Cure
Scriptural Text: John 11:25

<u>Insights for Meditation and Prayerful Application</u>
"**Prevention is better than cure**" is a popular saying in the world of medicine. However, while certain diseases can be prevented – like malaria, typhoid, osteoporosis, diabetes, hypertension, migraine, HIV/AIDS etc, there is one major disease which no man has been able to prevent in life; it is called DEATH. This disease doesn't care whether you take drugs regularly, eat balanced diets, and do regular medical check-ups or whether you are even a doctor yourself; it comes whenever it wants to come regardless of your various prevention therapies. However, there is good news; though this disease called death cannot be prevented in life, it can be cured. And that's the TOP SECRET. **The only Cure to death is "The Resurrection and the Life" – the One who swallowed up death in victory and took the keys of Death and Hades from the devil.** [John 11:25, Heb 2:14-15, John 5:28-29, Revelation 1:18, 1 Corinthians 15:54-55].

With Jesus- the Resurrection and the Life- reigning in your life and mortal body, the issue of death is automatically settled. For you, there are two ways to leave this world: one is through rapture and the other way is by falling asleep [1 Corinthians 15:35-55]. The first way is very beautiful, God just takes you as you are and relocates you to Paradise like the cases of Enoch and Elijah in Genesis 5:24 and 2Kings 2:11 respectively. All genuine Christians are waiting for this glorious event before the world eventually comes to an end. But if you fall asleep before then, which is the second way of departing from this world, there is still a cure. Jesus would raise you up again and your soul will be preserved from eternal destruction in the Lake of Fire which is the real (incurable) death. [Rev 20:11-15].

So if you are still alive, congratulations. Stop running to secret societies, covens of darkness, witch doctors, fake prayer houses, false prophets, juju priests, traditional groups etc all in the name of protection; trying to prevent death. I tell you the truth; these things will even hasten your untimely death. The only One who has the key of Death and Life is Jesus Christ. Accept Him into your life now and start living as He commanded in the Bible –live holy, obey Him, love your neighbours, fellowship with other believers in the church etc – then you will live forever. For you, the cure to death is in your pocket because with Jesus you have passed from death to life [John 11:25-26, 38-44; John 5:24].

"No Jesus, No Life"! And the absence of life is called DEATH [John 10:10].

Say this prayer now: *Dear Lord Jesus, I am a sinner. Please forgive me of all my sins, I accept you into my life today as my personal Lord and Saviour. Help me to live a holy life beginning from now, and keep me from Eternal Death. Thank you for saving me.*

Note: Keep meditating on these insights throughout this week and prayerfully apply them to relevant areas of your life and even those of others.

Prayer Focus: Say these prayers for each day as you meditate on the insights received.

Day 1: Father, thank You for the priceless gift of Your Son, Jesus Christ.

Day 2: Father by Your power, quicken every dead part of my body.

Day 3: Father, let my buried glory and blessings resurrect in the Name of Jesus.

Day 4: Father, please terminate any appointment I have with untimely death.

Day 5: Father, there is no one like You. Please show Your Almightiness in my favour.

Day 6: Father, please let the dry bones in my family and career rise again.

Day 7: Resurrection and the Life, please deliver me from eternal death.

Week Ten

Study Focus: Understanding Your Enemy's Strategy
Scriptural Text: Genesis 3:4-5

<u>Insights for Meditation and Prayerful Application</u>
"And the serpent said unto the woman, ye shall not surely die. For God doth know that in the day ye eat thereof, then your eyes shall be opened, and ye shall be as gods, knowing good and evil"- Gen 3:4-5 (KJV)
Beware of the devil, he doesn't show the two sides of the coin in all his temptations. He will always tell you one and cover/blind your eyes to the other.
In his discussion with Eve, he was right in saying they would have the knowledge of good and bad but he didn't tell her that the death God talked about was spiritual –eternal separation from Divinity. Verse 22 of Genesis chapter 3 confirms the serpent's claim that they would be like God in knowing good and bad, but he didn't present disobedience to her as a sin – and it is forever settled that the soul that sinneth shall die. Ezekiel 18:4.

In tempting a Christian, the devil may quote a part of the scripture but he will not give him the other side of the same scripture. For instance while tempting Jesus Christ in Matthew 4:5-6, he quoted Psalm 91:11-12 to Him but didn't mention Deuteronomy 6:16. He may decide to hold a Christian captive by quoting Isaiah 49:24, but the Christian will have to possess the understanding of verse 25 of the same Isaiah 49 to be free from him. Be very careful with him. Anytime you find yourself quoting scriptures to justify your sinful acts, it is the devil; quickly rebuke him in the Name of Jesus. Remember, your sins must be confessed (and not defended) for you to be forgiven – 1John 1:9, Proverbs 28:13.

Take time to study God's word so that you will always have an answer for him like Jesus did. There is no single truth in the devil; the Bible calls him the father of lies –John 8:44. Never say yes to devil's suggestions, it could be likened to a suicide mission. Accept Jesus now, and the power to always say no to the devil will be released to you. The Peace of the Lord be with you.

Note: Keep meditating on these insights throughout this week and prayerfully apply them to relevant areas of your life and even those of others.

Prayer Focus: Say these prayers for each day as you meditate on the insights received.
Day 1: Father, I reject all the lies of the devil over my life and family in Jesus' Name.
Day 2: Father, please silence the voice of the devil over my destiny.
Day 3: Father, please keep exposing my enemies' secrets to me.
Day 4: Father, let my enemies fall into the very traps they have set for me.
Day 5: Father, please frustrate all the plans of my adversaries against my future.
Day 6: Father, give me the grace to always be sober and vigilant.
Day 7: Father, please lead me not into temptation and deliver me from all evil.

Week Eleven

Study Focus: You Have a Choice
Scriptural Text: Deuteronomy 30:19

<u>Insights for Meditation and Prayerful Application</u>
Man was created with the ability to make choices. Unlike the lower animals, man has a highly developed mind which makes it very possible for him to discern the good and the bad as well as to choose between the two.
I have heard people say things like: *"I am easily provoked", "I have hot temper", "I find it difficult to forgive", "I get angry easily"* among other similar expressions. Although they feel they are simply being sincere and frank, such are not healthy for the soul; and this is where the power of choice comes in to get rid of such emotions.

For instance, as an adult, nobody forces you to take your bath and brush your teeth on a daily basis; you also eat when you feel hungry and you wear clothes based on your choices. It is actually the same with your emotions. You can decide which one to exhibit and which one to suppress. Your temper is your own, not any other person's; and you have the power to either lose it or keep it. Just as you have power over your teeth either to brush them or not, you have power over your temper as well. Nobody should be able to make you angry without your choice to become angry. You can choose to either lose your temper or hold it because it is your temper. It's simply a matter of choice.

When someone insults you, you can either choose to react or respond. If you choose to react, you will see yourself insulting the fellow as well, and if care is not taken, you might eventually engage the person in a physical fight which of course could lead to injuries or even manslaughter in severe cases. But if you choose to respond, all you need do is whisper to yourself "I refuse to be angry, may be this fellow is not in a right state of mind, or may be his day has not been fine or something related". You simply make excuses for his action because any normal fellow shouldn't take pleasure in insulting people just like that. By the time you finish pondering on all these possibilities in your mind, your temper would have cooled down and you would have saved yourself the stress of being engaged in a quarrel or a fight. It is such a lifestyle you can't afford to ignore. With this practice, nobody would ever be able to make you lose your temper. Even in a situation when you choose to be angry, it would be under control because you are conscious of it. Not the mad and destructive type that sets a house on fire before thinking of where the next accommodation would be. Always remember that your temper is your personal and legal possession, and no man on earth has the legitimate right to decide for you on what to do with it. You, and only you, have the power to do what you like with it. You can either lose it or hold it. The choice is yours!

Note: Keep meditating on these insights throughout this week and prayerfully apply them to relevant areas of your life and even those of others.

Prayer Focus: Say these prayers for each day as you meditate on the insights received.
Day 1: Father, please forgive me for all the wrong choices I have made in life.
Day 2: Father please by Your mercy deliver me from the consequences of wrong choices.
Day 3: Father, please give me the grace to make the right choices from now on.
Day 4: Father, please help me to always be positive and stay positive.
Day 5: Powers manipulating my mind, your time is up. Get out of my life in Jesus' Name.

Day 6: Father, please let my victory over anger, unforgiving spirit and bitterness be total.

Day 7: Father, please be glorified in my thoughts, words and actions in Jesus' Name.

Week Twelve

Study Focus: Go Forward
Scriptural Text: Exodus 14:15

Insights for Meditation and Prayerful Application

After 430 years of slavery in the land of Egypt, the Israelites finally got their liberation and started towards the land God promised their ancestors under the leadership of Moses. It was a very glorious moment for them and they were so sure of their deliverance, even as verse 8b of Exodus 14 confirmed it. It says "...and the children of Israel went out with boldness". Boldness indicates confidence, so they were very convinced about their freedom. But suddenly, they lifted their eyes and behold the entire host of Egypt led by Pharaoh their arch enemy were pursuing them. At this time, their boldness turned to fear. Verse 10 says "...they were very afraid..." If they were to run faster so as to escape the attack; it would have been a good idea; but behold, there was Red Sea ahead of them - without any ship or bridge to cross them over. Realizing their doom, they murmured against Moses and cried to God in despair. Moses encouraged them but also cried to God.

Now, what was the Lord's reply under this life threatening situation? God simply said to Moses in verses 15-16 "Why do you cry to Me? Tell the children of Israel to go forward. But lift up your rod, and stretch out your hand over the sea and divide it. And the children of Israel shall go on dry ground through the midst of the sea". Moses obeyed the Lord and in verses 22 and 30, the Bible says "So, the children of Israel went into the midst of the sea on the dry ground, and the waters were a wall to them on their right hand and on their left. So the Lord saved Israel that day out of the hand of the Egyptians, and Israel saw the Egyptians dead on the seashore". In the next chapter, they sang a new song.

Now, what is the implication of this in your life as a believer?
The Egyptian force coming behind you represents what you have been delivered from or what you have shared testimony about; what you believed you're free from - they are coming after you again; and suddenly you become confused, saying to God - why this again, Lord? What am I going to do? Why is my testimony becoming a prayer point again? But listen to what the Lord of Hosts is saying: "Fear not, neglect, disregard and ignore them; they are not real, they are just like a toothless barking dog, it can't bite. You are seeing them now but by the time you look again, you'll never see them. Why? Because I will fulfill my word that is forever settled in Nahum 1:9 - "What do ye imagine against the Lord? He will make an utter (total, full, complete and permanent) end; affliction shall not rise up the second time" (*emphasis mine*). All you need do is just move FORWARD, don't mind them, stop crying, don't even pray about them, just GO FORWARD. I'll personally take care of them. "For instance, I've delivered you from headache and now you are feeling the symptoms again, don't mind it; it's just a feeling and I'll make an utter end of it in such a way that you'll never know what it means to have headache again. Just go forward - go on with your normal activities, don't pray about it, don't confess it, don't worry about taking drugs, it's not real; just ignore it and go on with your life. Tell it I said I'll make an utter end of it and that it'll not come the second time. You can also tell it I said I'll fight for you while you hold your peace and having said that; continue with your journey. In a moment, you'll look for it but not be able to find it - Isaiah 41:12-13.

And for the Red Sea waiting as a barrier before you; don't worry as well; just GO FORWARD. Don't stop. Pretend as if you are not seeing the obstacle to your progress. Before you get there or even on getting there, I WILL MAKE A WAY. Don't allow the obstacle to stop you from afar, approach it, keep travelling towards it; before it stops you, I'll part it. Did you remember my daughters, Mary Magdalene, Mary the mother of James and Salome in Mark 16:1-6? They wanted to gain access to where I was laid, but were thinking and worrying among themselves who would help them roll away the stone covering the entrance; for it was a large stone. But you know what? Before they got there, My Father had already sent an angel to roll away the stone, so their worry was not necessary. Note this however, although they didn't know how the stone would be rolled away, yet they kept going forward; they didn't go back. That's GOING FORWARD.

Also consider the four lepers in 2 Kings 7:3-8. They went forward despite the army capable of wasting them; but before they got to the enemy's camp, the army had fled because the Lord made their feet sound like chariots of war - as if they were hired from neighbouring countries. But for God to magnify their steps, they first had to move. Ignore your "what ifs' - doubts, fear, analysis, reports, forecasts etc - JUST GO FORWARD. I still have the power to part your own Red Sea. For instance, a company needs a second class upper qualification from applicants to occupy a particular post. You saw the advert and all you have is second class lower; don't worry; if you like the job, apply, write the exams, go to the office, express your interest - keep advancing. Just at the point your lower qualification would be a barrier, I will step in and part the Red Sea for you to scale through. Always remember that until you step into Jordan, it will not part - Joshua 3:15-17. "If you wait for perfect conditions, you will never get anything done" - Ecclesiastes 11:4 (TLB). **JUST GO FORWARD!**

Note: Keep meditating on these insights throughout this week and prayerfully apply them to relevant areas of your life and even those of others.

Prayer Focus: Say these prayers for each day as you meditate on the insights received.

Day 1: Every power keeping me in perpetual bondage, be destroyed in Jesus' Name.

Day 2: Father, please remove every obstacle and barrier to my peaceful settlement.

Day 3: Father, let all my stubborn pursuers perish in Jesus' Name.

Day 4: Father, please let all my afflictions end now.
Day 5: Father, please put my fear in my enemies' hearts.
Day 6: Father, please liberate me and my family from ancestral slavery.
Day 7: Father, please don't allow our testimonies to become prayer points again.

Week Thirteen

Study Focus: Why Did This Happen To Me?
Scriptural Text: Job 1:1, 13-19

Insights for Meditation and Prayerful Application

Here is the most common question of the day, and perhaps it is the one question that is uppermost in your own mind at this very moment. Maybe sickness has come into your life with its suffering, its expenses and its gnawing uncertainty. Or again, it could be that death has struck your family circle with its own peculiar sorrow. Perhaps it is an accident that has upset your most cherished plans, or family strife that has brought misery and unhappiness into your home. Possibly your fondest dreams have been shattered by tragedy, debt or unemployment. For some reason or other, you are despondent, worried, nervous and ill. You wonder if life is worth living, and ask yourself, repeatedly, "Why did God let this happen to me?"

It is a good question to ask, and, incidentally, it is the only sane approach to finding the answer to your present difficulty. You could adopt the attitude of bold defiance, of course, and grimly determine to fight against your trials. Or you could just give up with the fatalistic attitude that your troubles are unavoidable anyway. But the best policy is to ask yourself quietly and calmly,

"Why did God allow this to come into my life?"

Your first temptation might be to reason that God is punishing you for some sin that you have committed. While this could very possibly be true, it is obviously not the principal reason for your distress. If God's main purpose were punishment, He could have taken your life away altogether. Instead of that, He has purposely extended your life so that your question might be answered. "Why," you ask, "did this happen to me?"

The answer is that God wants to speak to you. He has tried to speak to you before, but as long as things were going well with you, you weren't interested in listening. He knows that the only way to get your attention is to allow trials to come into your life. He is so interested in you that He is even willing to permit you to suffer for a short time if only as a result you might be made happy forever.

God has four purposes for you in these trials.
First of all, He wants you to feel your need for help.
Secondly, He wants you to realise your inability to help yourself. Again, He wants you to abandon all hope of obtaining relief from your fellow men.
Finally, He wants you to cast yourself on Him and ask Him to save you. You see, if you had died before now, you would have been lost throughout all eternity. Your sins have never been forgiven, and because of this, you would have been barred from Heaven forever.

But God does not want you to perish. In order that He might have an honourable way of forgiving your sins, He sent His Son, the Lord Jesus, to die on the Cross of Calvary. Christ died for ungodly sinners so that they might be forgiven. Three days after His burial, the Saviour rose again, and then some time later, He went back to Heaven, where He is at this very moment, waiting to save you.

Now here is the message which God is trying to make you understand. If you will acknowledge your sins and receive the Son of God as your Lord and Saviour, He will forgive your sins and give you eternal life in Heaven. He has definitely promised this in His Word, the Holy Bible, and He cannot go back on His promise.

"Verily, verily, I say unto you, he that believeth on me hath everlasting life" (John's Gospel, Chapter 6, verse 47).

The great question which you must face just now is this, "Will I or will I not open the door of my heart and welcome the Lord as my Saviour?" If you refuse Him, you will only go out to face further sorrow and disappointment in this life, and everlasting woe in the next.

If you receive Him, you will be given strength to bear every trial and testing on earth, and will be guaranteed unending joy in Heaven.
No matter how severe your troubles are just now, they would be well worth every throbbing pain.

Note: Keep meditating on these insights throughout this week and prayerfully apply them to relevant areas of your life and even those of others.

Prayer Focus: Say these prayers for each day as you meditate on the insights received.

Day 1: Father, thank You for every experience You have allowed to come into my life.

Day 2: Father in areas I have fallen short of Your glory, please forgive and restore me.

Day 3: Father please by Your mercy, take away all my reproach.

Day 4: Father, please increase my level of trust in You.

Day 5: Father, please let my weeping come to an end. Replace my sorrow with Your joy.

Day 6: Father, I will serve You till the very end. Please uphold me by Your grace.

Day 7: Father, I thank You because I know all my experiences are working for my good.

Week Fourteen

Study Focus: Life Applicable Lessons from the Book of Ruth [Part I]
Scriptural Text: Ruth 1: 1-22

Insights for Meditation and Prayerful Application

As we deeply study the Book of Ruth, some truths become so important for us to consider. Firstly, as a man, you must learn to take responsibility for your family. Elimelech discovered there was famine in the land which threatened the continued existence of his family. He didn't just sit down in despair; he took a drastic action by finding out where there was food and relocating his family there for sustenance. That's being a responsible husband and father.

Also, we noticed that Naomi, his wife, didn't come up with a contrary vision. She simply complied with her head's instruction and gravitated towards his direction. It was the duty of the man to provide direction for the family and as a responsible wife, she cooperated with her husband. As a result of this demonstration of unity of purpose, their children –Mahlon and Chilion - had no option than to follow suit. When the father plays his role and the mother supports without rebelling, their children will definitely be cooperative. For instance, if the father declares the God of Israel as the God his family will worship and his wife complies, the children will not follow Baal. However, the man must take the lead before expecting his family to follow. He must have a vision for the family which his wife and children are to pursue with him. [Ruth 1: 1-2].

Secondly, bad times also happen to God's people. Famine – an extreme scarcity of food – visited God's own people. In Bethlehem, a place known and named as 'the house of bread', there was no bread. Despite being connected to Judah –which means 'praise', their condition was not praiseworthy but life-threatening. There is no level of relationship with God that will keep certain unfavourable situations like famine away permanently. It was recorded in Gen 12:10 that there was a famine in the time of Abraham (despite his close relationship with God), and another one in the time of his son Isaac (Gen 26:1). Their faithful and covenant walk with God couldn't prevent famine from coming. However, according to 1 Corinthians 10:13, He had always made a way out for His own. In Gen 41:29-36 for instance, God warned Egypt of an imminent famine through the dream He gave to Pharaoh. He thereafter gave Joseph the wisdom to apply in order to scale through the famine without being hurt by it. It simply follows that though bad times (famine) are inevitable as long as this earth exists, they can be wisely planned for in order to come out of them victoriously. [Ruth 1:1].

Thirdly, no condition is permanent. Even if there is famine today, God will visit you with bread once again as recorded in Ruth 1: 6. According to Ecclesiastes 3: 1-8, there is a time for everything under the heavens. If you are in your season of famine now, be very confident that it will soon give way to your season of plenty. Conversely, if you are at present enjoying abundance; be assured that a time of scarcity is also coming. So you must plan to welcome it when it comes. With this consciousness, every season of life should be treated with utmost wisdom. Plenty is not permanent, so you must invest; and famine is not permanent, so you must be courageous to scale through while it lasts. In the case of Egypt, the famine lasted only seven (7) years –Gen 41:29-36, while in the case of Judah, Naomi heard after about ten (10) years that the famine had ended. No famine is eternal as far as this earth is concerned.

Fourthly, regardless of the kinds of blow the world has dealt or is at present dealing you, never sit down in defeat. Arise and head towards a new beginning. Attempt a fresh start. Acknowledge your unfortunate situation, don't deny it; but never accept it as the conclusion of your condition. In verse 6 of Ruth chapter 1, despite all the woes that had befallen Naomi, she arose and headed for a new beginning. Even if you have fallen up to seven times, God expects you to get up and keep going - Proverbs 24:10, 16.

Fifthly, tenacity (perseverance) is a vital ingredient for destiny fulfillment. This virtue played out in Ruth 1: 14-18 as Ruth refused to be persuaded against her destiny. She saw something in Naomi's family which was totally different from what her background portrayed and she decided to cling unto that. All effort to derail her was abortive as she tenaciously held on to her resolution. Her sister-in-law decided to yield after a little persuasion but not Ruth. She was willing to die for what she believed in and according to Matthew 1:5, her tenacity was rewarded as she found herself named among those Jesus Christ, the King of kings descended from. Jacob also exhibited this kind of tenacity in Gen 32:26 and he had his destiny transformed forever.

Sixthly, never blame your circumstances on God. God is always good. Elimelech died, Mahlon and Chilion also died, leaving Naomi alone. Yet she didn't see the fact that her being the only survivor is God's goodness. She was so clouded with her challenges that she described her condition as God's Hand afflicting her. She attributed all her woes to God being against her – Ruth 1: 19-22. God is the One to run to in times of trouble, not the One to blame. He is good to all (Psalm 145:9, Matthew 5:45). Look for the good Hand of God in all your circumstances. Blaming God only keeps you in perpetual defeat.

Note: Keep meditating on these insights throughout this week and prayerfully apply them to relevant areas of your life and even those of others.

Prayer Focus: Say these prayers for each day as you meditate on the insights received.
Day 1: Father, grant all our parents the grace to take responsibility for their families.
Day 2: Father, please grant me the grace to overcome the challenging moments of life.
Day 3: Father, please let the tides of life begin to turn in my favour.

Day 4: Father regardless of my present challenges, please give me a new beginning.

Day 5: Father, please release upon me the tenacity needed to fulfill my destiny.

Day 6: Father, I know You are always good. Let me never blame my challenges on You.

Day 7: Father, I thank You for the beautiful plans You have for my future.

Week Fifteen

Study Focus: Life Applicable Lessons from the Book of Ruth [Part II]
Scriptural Text: Ruth 2: 1-23

Insights for Meditation and Prayerful Application

Firstly, regardless of your mighty connections within and outside your family, until God decides to help you, you won't be helped – Ruth 2:1, 20.

Elimelech had a kinsman described as *a mighty man of wealth*, yet he was so affected by the famine in the land that he had to relocate his nuclear family to Moab. Benefitting from the wealth of Boaz could have cushioned the effect on him but he wasn't a partaker at the time. In 2Kings 6: 26-27, the king of Israel said *'...if the Lord do not help thee, whence shall I help thee...?* By implication, it means your uncle's prosperity or your friend's connection with the highly placed may not be the cure to your unemployment or poverty. You may be surrounded by helpers, I mean those with the solution to your problems; but until the Lord moves them to help you, your struggle continues. God can even use strangers to help you like He raised Ruth, a Moabitess, to help Naomi – Ruth 2:2. Get this once and for all, **only God can help you** (Psalm 121:1-2).

Secondly, action precedes favour. You must do what you can before God will do what you can't – Ruth 2:2-3.

It has been said that the faith that expects God to do everything is an irresponsible faith. God expects you to make efforts before backing you up; He doesn't work with zero efforts. Before He killed Goliath, He needed David to engage the sling (1 Samuel 17); before He parted the Red Sea, He needed Moses to engage the rod (Exodus 14); before He delivered the nations into the hands of Israel, He needed Joshua to engage the sword (Joshua 10); before He collapsed the wall of Jericho, He needed the Israelites to give a shout (Joshua 6); before sending the Messiah, He needed Mary to keep her virginity (Luke 1); and before showing Ruth and Naomi favour through Boaz, He needed Ruth to get out of the house and go out to glean (Ruth 2:2-3). Boaz didn't come to their house, they met on the field. So, if Ruth had remained in the house, she might have missed that God-ordained favour.

You need a job, but you won't go out to search; all you do is complain. Even if there is favour waiting for you somewhere, your sitting down at home will rob you of it.

Always do what your strength can still do, and you will see God doing what your strength cannot carry. At that time, you will experience His favour.

Thirdly, according to Ruth 2:4, how many employers attract "God bless you" from their employees? That is something every employer must think about. Boaz's servants blessed him. The way you are treating your employees, can they really bless you? Also, as employees, do you see your work as a blessing from God? Hope you are aware that many are jobless? Such thinking should make you overflow with gratitude to your employer. Boaz blessed these servants by engaging them in his harvest, thereby qualifying them for some income. And upon his arrival to check what they were doing, they greeted him by saying **"The Lord bless thee"**.

Fourthly, you reap what you sow – Ruth 2:10. Ruth showed favour to Naomi, a stranger, in Moab; and she reaped favour as a stranger in Israel. What goes round still comes round. Treat others the way you want to be treated so that your harvest will not fill your mouth with bitter pills (Matthew 7:12).

Fifthly, when you appreciate little kindness, you get greater kindness. In verses 8-10, Ruth appreciated the kindness Boaz showed her, and by the time we got to verses 14-17, we saw her enjoying greater favour. Take note of this as well, your attitude is being noticed whether you are aware or not. Somehow, some unseen eyes of men are watching your attitude (verses 11-12); so you can't really hide your attitude.

Sixthly, favour may sometimes mean more work. To appreciate the source of the favour therefore, you must be willing to engage the favour through hardwork. According to chapter 2, Ruth was favoured by being given more stuff to glean which she diligently did until the evening. God may open a door for you as a favour, but you must be ready to walk through the door and fully explore the opportunity. And that means more work is needed. So, if you are not ready for hardwork, stop praying for God's favour.

Quickly say this prayer: Father, you are the One who raised Ruth to help Naomi in her helpless state, please raise loyal helpers for me too. Helpers who will not stop helping me no matter what, raise them for me now in Jesus' Name.

Note: Keep meditating on these insights throughout this week and prayerfully apply them to relevant areas of your life and even those of others.

Prayer Focus: Say these prayers for each day as you meditate on the insights received.

Day 1: Father, I know vain is the help of man. Please be my present help in time of need.

Day 2: Father the action I need to take to provoke Your favour, please help me to take it.

Day 3: Father, let me begin to reap all the good seeds You have helped me to sow.

Day 4: Father I receive wisdom to appreciate little acts of kindness to get greater ones.

Day 5: Father, help me to never receive Your favour and grace in vain.

Day 6: Father, please teach me Your Ways.

Day 7: Father, please let Your good Hand always be upon me and my family.

Week Sixteen

Study Focus: Be Still
Scriptural Text: Psalm 46:10

<u>**Insights for Meditation and Prayerful Application**</u>
When it comes to obtaining assistance from God concerning any issue of concern, only Him is permitted to be awake. If you are asking Him for help and you are still fully awake, struggling and making anxious efforts at getting the problems solved, He will keep 'sleeping' (remain inactive) until you are exhausted. But if you wake Him up like His disciples did when the storm was threatening their lives in Mark 4:35-39 and choose to be still while He works on your behalf, you will soon be sharing testimonies. He told the Israelites through Moses to be still and before they knew what was happening, the Red Sea had parted. Also, Adam had to be put to rest while God worked on his problem of loneliness. Please stop hindering God by your anxious moves; to enjoy His Intervention, you will have to BE STILL AND KNOW THAT HE IS GOD!

Note: Keep meditating on these insights throughout this week and prayerfully apply them to relevant areas of your life and even those of others.

Prayer Focus: Say these prayers for each day as you meditate on the insights received.
Day 1: Father, I give You praise for all Your beautiful promises.
Day 2: Father, please speak Your peace to every storm of my life.

Day 3: Father, please arise on my behalf and let the enemies of my peace be scattered.

Day 4: I receive grace to live a worry-free life from today in the Name of Jesus.

Day 5: Father, this very day, please make a way for me where there is no way.

Day 6: Oh you raging storm blowing against my well-being, cease in the Name of Jesus.

Day 7: Father, please for the rest of my life, keep me and my family in perfect peace.

Week Seventeen

Study Focus: A True Life Story
Scriptural Text: Mark 5: 25-34

Insights for Meditation and Prayerful Application

Several years ago, there was a certain woman who suffered a serious haemorrhagic condition. She bled so heavily that her case became a concern. It all happened that while she was growing up as a girl, she reached the age of puberty and started menstruating as it is normal with girls of her age. She would have her monthly period and after some days it would cease till the following month. She kept growing and going about her life as a normal person, full of dreams and aspirations. She worked so hard and became a woman of substance, having a great fortune. She could simply be described as rich and her life was going on beautifully well. However, a day came; she saw her menses (monthly discharge) and adjusted her body as usual to accommodate the blood flow for the few days it would run. But to her surprise, the menses that had not taken more than 5 – 6 days before started extending. The blood flow continued for one week, two weeks, three weeks, four weeks and was even entering the 12th week when she decided to seek medical assistance. And because she could afford it, she engaged the services of sound physicians.

They ran several tests on her, after which they gave her some medications to help solve her problem. She took the drugs prescribed for her religiously with the hope of getting better, but to her surprise the bleeding got worse as the flow became heavier. Out of desperation, she decided to try other medical specialists who after several abortive efforts referred her to a Consultant Heamatologist – who specializes in blood related disorders. At this time, her problem was no longer a matter of months but years. People had started avoiding her company; all her friends had deserted her because they just couldn't fathom what was responsible for her infirmity. She couldn't go about her business again because nobody was willing to transact any business with her due to the offensive odour emanating from her body. She was a complete mess and was merely living on the money she had managed to save while she was still healthy. On meeting this Consultant Haematologist, her hopes were so high that even when she discovered that his bill would cost her all she had left to live on, she didn't mind. She made all the money available to the man to commence treatment believing that once she became fine, she would work and earn money again. The Consultant commenced her treatment and displayed all his expertise acquired over the years. He did all he could but unfortunately, the woman's case got worsened. She was given few more weeks to live as her continuous loss of blood would eventually terminate her life.

Disappointed, frustrated and sad, this woman returned home and hopelessly retired to fate. "Come to think of it' she said, "I am alone in all this, no man will marry a bleeding woman, no organization will employ a bleeding woman, socially I have become unacceptable, medical personnel have failed me, all my means of livelihood gone and I have been given few more weeks to live. Well, I will just sit down and wait for the inevitable death" she concluded.

It was now 12 good years that her blood had been flowing ceaselessly. One day, as she was still hopelessly waiting for her final moment she heard of someone talking about a man named Jesus who recently drove out 6,000 demons from a mad man. She also heard that this Jesus could heal any sickness and cure any disease. Upon hearing this, a little ray of hope rose within her. But then she heard that it was very difficult to reach Him because of the crowd who always went about with Him. At this point, she became sad again because she had lost so much blood and had become too weak to struggle with any crowd. Also, her smelling condition would not allow the multitude to be at home with her presence. But then she thought of something, she said "I would try and go to this Jesus; I wouldn't struggle with the crowd, all I would do is just touch the hem of his clothes and I believe upon doing that, I will be well again". So she arose and went. And true to the report she heard, a lot of crowd was with Jesus; but she tried and made her way through to touch the hem of His clothes as she had purposed. And guess what? Immediately she did that, her 12 years ceaseless bleeding which no medical expertise could cure stopped, because power flowed from Jesus' garment into her body and she became fine right there with all her hopes, dreams and aspirations restored. The power she contacted from Jesus not only healed her, but also delivered her from death and gave her reasons to live again. Praise God!

This story was extracted from Mark 5:25 – 34. And the good news is this; the Jesus who attended to this woman is still alive today and forever more with the same power and ability. (Hebrews 13:8). Your own problem may not be related to bleeding; but remember, **He heals ALL sicknesses and cures ALL diseases.** Just go to Him like that woman and touch Him by faith, you will surely testify.

Say this prayer now: *Dear Lord Jesus, I am a sinner. Please forgive me of all my sins, I accept you into my life today as my personal Lord and Saviour. Write my name in the Book of Life, help me to live a holy life beginning from now, and please solve all my problems. Thank you for saving me. Hallelujah!*

Note: Keep meditating on these insights throughout this week and prayerfully apply them to relevant areas of your life and even those of others.

Prayer Focus: Say these prayers for each day as you meditate on the insights received.
Day 1: Lord Jesus, thank You for the power in Your Blood.
Day 2: Blood of Jesus, begin to speak in my favour.
Day 3: Father, please terminate every shameful experience in my life.
Day 4: Father, please uproot every source of reproach in my life and family.
Day 5: Father, please grant me the grace to grow in faith.
Day 6: Father, let my long awaited testimonies appear speedily.

Day 7: Father, please replace all my sorrows with Your abundant joy.

Week Eighteen

Study Focus: Is Banana The Same As Plantain?
Scriptural Text: Luke 6:43-45

Insights for Meditation and Prayerful Application

Have you ever considered how difficult it is to differentiate between banana and plantain plants? Their stems look alike, their leaves look alike, they thrive in the same environment, and sometimes even have similar heights. Quite a number of people have confused banana plant for plantain by mere looking at them. However, there is only one major thing that doesn't look alike in both plants; and that is their "FRUITS". Both plants may generate confusion in the minds of observers for a while, but the moment fruiting commences, all doubts will be gone.

In the same vein, anyone can claim to be a child of God, a Pastor, a Prophet, an Evangelist, a Bishop or even a General Overseer. They may even look like what they claim by carrying big and intimidating Bibles, wearing serious looking suits, being in charge of big churches with large congregations or some may even be performing unusual miracles; and observers will be persuaded that truly, these men are from God. That is the deception of Plantain and Banana. In order to know which of them is from God, **LOOK OUT FOR THEIR FRUITS, NOT THEIR WORKS, TITLES OR APPEARANCE.** Luke 6:43 -45 says "...every tree is known by its own fruit..." *not by its looks.*

Matthew 7:21-23 says many people with good works like prophesying, casting out devils among other wonderful works (but without good fruits) will be denied by the Lord Jesus and consequently be shut out of Heaven.

Look at your own life and check if your fruits look like the ones in Galatians 5:22 (love, joy, peace etc); if they are similar, congratulations. With or without any church title or big anointing, your eternity in Heaven is secured. But if your fruits look like those in Galatians 5: 19 – 21 (adultery, fornication, envy, drunkenness, hatred etc), you are already on your way to Hell regardless of your big church title, anointing or anything you feel you are doing for God.

Similarly, before you submit your spiritual life to any man or woman of God for mentorship or grooming, watch the fruits at work in his/her life. Don't look at the number of people worshiping in their churches or the kinds of miracles they are performing; **LOOK FOR THE FRUITS!** This is how to be delivered from False Prophets and also be prevented from becoming one yourself. Heaven and Hell are still real! WATCH! (Mark 13:37).

Oh, you may now want to ask; how then can I begin to bear good fruits? That's quite simple; just change your ROOTS. Matthew 12:33 says if you make a tree good, the fruits also will become good. Repent of your sinful ways, ask the Lord Jesus (the custodian of good fruits) to come into your life and start feeding on His Word (the Bible). The fruits will develop, it's GUARANTEED!

Note: Keep meditating on these insights throughout this week and prayerfully apply them to relevant areas of your life and even those of others.

Prayer Focus: Say these prayers for each day as you meditate on the insights received.
Day 1: Father, please take away every bad attitude from my life.
Day 2: Father, please empower me to bear good fruits.
Day 3: Father, destroy every work of darkness in my life and family.
Day 4: Father, from now on, let my life begin to give You glory.
Day 5: Father, please deliver me from the deception of men.
Day 6: Father, let Your judgment come upon every unrepentant false prophet.

Day 7: Father, no matter what happens, let me reign with You in Your Kingdom.

Week Nineteen

Study Focus: Why Did Elijah Run?
Scriptural Text: I Kings 19:1-3

<u>**Insights for Meditation and Prayerful Application**</u>
In 1 Kings 19:1-3(KJV), we read of King Ahab narrating the Mount Carmel experience which led to the slaughter of the Prophets of Baal by Elijah to his (satanic) wife –Jezebel. Upon hearing this report, Jezebel, who had no regard for the God of Israel let alone Elijah, became furious and sent a "message" to Elijah saying by the following day, she was going to kill him just the way he had killed those Baal Prophets. Now notice that was a message to be delivered to Elijah, and Elijah was going to hear the message with his ears. The messenger arrived and delivered Jezebel's message to Elijah. Elijah actually heard the message firsthand from the messenger. But the Bible says in verse 3, "And when he (Elijah) saw that, he arose, and went for his life…" Words were spoken to Elijah, but he saw pictures and he ran. This is the same Elijah who killed 450 powerful Baal Prophets just about 24hours ago.

Elijah didn't run because of the message from Jezebel, rather he ran because of what he saw in the process of meditating on what he heard.

It is very important to note that words can become pictures in the mind. Negative words should never be allowed to become pictures (through the process of meditation).We are enjoined to gird up the loins of our mind (1Peter 1:13). This means we are to take full responsibility of what is allowed into our minds as well as what goes on there.

The mere fact that the government announced some food stuffs as likely breeding grounds for Lassa fever doesn't mean you will contact the disease if you consume them. It's just a caution.

Simply because a particular road has been described as prone to accidents doesn't mean you shouldn't travel through there or that you should expect to have an accident when you take that road. It's just a report. You don't have to think on everything you hear. Before you meditate or process any words in your mind, they must pass the Philippians 4:8 test (please read). That is the only way to generate positive pictures in your mind.

It is therefore not what you hear that determines your action or reaction; it is what you make out of what you hear. Guard your thoughts!

Note: Keep meditating on these insights throughout this week and prayerfully apply them to relevant areas of your life and even those of others.

Prayer Focus: Say these prayers for each day as you meditate on the insights received.

Day 1: In the Name of Jesus, I curse every Jezebel assigned to frustrate my destiny.

Day 2: My testimonies will never become prayer points again in the Name of Jesus.

Day 3: Every activity of demons in my life ceases now in the Name of Jesus.

Day 4: I sanctify my thoughts in the Name of Jesus.

Day 5: I destroy every negative picture bombarding my mind in Jesus' Name.

Day 6: Arrows of bad news sent against me, go back to sender in Jesus' Name.

Day 7: I refuse to fail and I refuse to be confused, I will fulfill my destiny in Jesus' Name.

Week Twenty

Study Focus: Really Believe In Jesus? You Need This Information
Scriptural Text: Mark 4: 35-39

Insights for Meditation and Prayerful Application

A close look at Mark 4: 35-39 presents certain facts every believer in Christ should take note of. Jesus Christ had just said to His disciples *"Let us cross over unto the other side"*. But between the time this statement was made and its actual fulfillment in Mark 5:1, something happened. The Bible says a great storm of wind arose and the waves beat into their ship. And from this we learn the following lessons:

1. Storms of life usually come uninvited and without prior notice. You just never can tell when a storm will arise. Mark 4:37.
2. Between where you are and where you want to be or are destined to be in life, you must encounter storms. That is, between the pronouncement and the fulfillment of your prophecies, storms must arise. Let us cross over to the other side (verse 35) was a prophecy – where they were going; but before they got there in Mark 5:1, there was a storm (Chapter 4 verse 37).
3. The Presence of God in your life will not prevent storms from arising in your life; however His Presence is your guarantee that you will overcome the storm. This means no level of spirituality will keep storms away; you are only assured of victory. Jesus was physically present in the ship, yet the storm arose (chapter 4 verses 35-39), John 2: 1-11, 2Kings 6:1-7.
4. To benefit from His Presence however, you must "wake Him up" (chapter 4 verse 38). Even though He is in your boat, He

won't intervene unless you consciously wake Him up or turn to Him for help. Until they woke Him up, He was still sleeping despite the great storm. Until they asked Him for help in John 2, He didn't turn their water to wine. James 4:2c says ye have not because ye ask not. Don't assume God will do something about your problem because He knows about it; He wants you to wake Him up through your prayers, worship, praises, sacrificial giving, meditating on His Word and putting Him in remembrance of what he had said concerning you in His Word.

5. Note that he rebuked His disciples for their unbelief in verse 40; He expected them to have held on to His word which he told them before the journey began. He had told them "Let us cross over to the other side". The storm was a mere distraction but they saw it as "carest not that we perish?" When the Lord tells you anything, He expects you to believe it and consider it done regardless of the storm that may arise (Psalm 33:8-9). That is His expectation from us as believers. Focus on what He had said, the storm is a mere distraction. **HIS WORDS MUST SURELY COME TO PASS, HE WILL NEVER NEVER LIE!**

Note: Keep meditating on these insights throughout this week and prayerfully apply them to relevant areas of your life and even those of others.

Prayer Focus: Say these prayers for each day as you meditate on the insights received.

Day 1: I shield my life and family from every storm of life in the Name of Jesus.

Day 2: I crush every barrier to the fulfillment of my prophecies in Jesus' Name.

Day 3: Father, please let Your Presence continually abide with me and my family.

Day 4: Father, arise and turn my darkness to light.

Day 5: Father, don't let Your words fall to the ground over my life.

Day 6: Father, destroy every sign of unbelief in my heart. Please help my faith.

Day 7: I am victorious over every storm of life in the Name of Jesus.

Week Twenty-One

Study Focus: Operating the Covenant of Divine Partnership
Scriptural Text: Ruth 3:3-4

Insights for Meditation and Prayerful Application

In the Book of Ruth, we see the Principle of Divine Partnership as it played out in the life of Ruth. In Ruth 3:-3-4, God used Naomi to give Ruth some specific instructions capable of generating a new beginning in her life despite the loss of her husband in Moab. The instructions were meant to settle her for life if carried out. Naomi told her to wash herself, anoint herself, put on her best garment, and go down to the threshing floor without making herself known to the man (Boaz) until he has finished eating and drinking. Thereafter, she was to notice where the man lay and go there to uncover his feet and lay there. In verse 5, Ruth promised to do all her mother-in-law had told her. In my opinion, that was a decision to cooperate with the helper of her destiny. She did all, and by the time she returned and told her mother-in-law how she had done all, Naomi told her to sit down and watch how things would turn out in her favour (verse 18). Naomi assured her that Boaz would not rest until he had tidied all that was necessary for her to become settled in life. By the time we got to chapter 4, we noticed that true to Naomi's assertion, Boaz left no stone unturned towards securing Ruth's destiny. In verse 13 of chapter 4, Ruth became settled as Boaz's wife and God honoured her so much to the extent of making our Lord Jesus Christ, the Son of David descend from her ancestral line. As a matter of fact, all is indeed well that ends well.

Lesson: God is your Greatest Helper and it is your responsibility to get instructions from Him through His Word, Visions, Prophets, Pastors etc towards getting your prayers answered. Once you are told what to do, cooperate with Him by going ahead to do it. The moment you are sure you have carried out those instructions of His, you are free to "sit" down, joyfully and thankfully expecting your answers. Just like Boaz, without your knowing or further input, He will do all that is necessary to get your answers delivered to you. That is the Divine Order towards enjoying answered prayers. **You do your part and He responds by doing His part.** For example, you pay your tithe, He rebukes the devourers for you and pours out a blessing on you (Malachi 3:10-12); you honour Him with your first fruit, He fills your barns (stores) with abundance (Proverbs 3:9-10) etc. You are not permitted to experience His part until your part is taken care of. That is how to operate the **Covenant of Divine Partnership.** I invite you to sign up, it's free for Believers.

Note: Keep meditating on these insights throughout this week and prayerfully apply them to relevant areas of your life and even those of others.

Prayer Focus: Say these prayers for each day as you meditate on the insights received.

Day 1: I receive grace to obey divine instructions from now on in the Name of Jesus.

Day 2: Father, from the four corners of the earth, please send help to me.

Day 3: Covenant keeping God, manifest Yourself in my family today.

Day 4: In the Name of Jesus, there shall be no losses in my life.

Day 5: I declare my family sickness and affliction free in the Name of Jesus.

Day 6: Father, I embrace Your covenant of divine partnership from today.

Day 7: Lord Jesus, please flood my heart with Your love.

Week Twenty-Two

Study Focus: The List with Only Two Sections
Scriptural Text: John 3:16-18

<u>Insights for Meditation and Prayerful Application</u>
The Titanic was presumed to be the largest, safest and strongest luxury ship in the world before it embarked on its disastrous maiden voyage in April 1912.
All kinds of people were welcomed on the ship for its first voyage. The rich, the famous, the elite, women, children, families and staff of the ship were all happy to be on board.
It was billed to be the ship that could not sink, but it did sink on its first journey from Southampton to New York.
This was one of the greatest tragedies of all time.
After the ship sank, two lists were presented at the offices of The White Star Company (the company which built the Titanic). The list was simple.
It had only two sections: **'LOST'** and **'SAVED'**.
People came to read these lists to find out if their loved ones had survived. Interestingly, before the journey so many things were important.
Whether they worked on the ship or were on vacation?
Whether they were rich or poor.
Whether they were millionaires or peasants.
Whether they were stockbrokers or not.
Whether they were in first class or economy class.
Whether they were men or women.
Whether they had a lot of luggage or not.

But after the sinking of the Titanic none of these things mattered anymore. Only one thing mattered – whether they were saved or lost.

Dear friend that is how Eternity will be.

A time will come when none of the things we have on this earth will matter.

A time will come when it will not matter whether you are a man or a woman, rich or poor!

What will matter is whether you are **'LOST'** or **'SAVED'** on the day you die and meet your Creator.

GIVE YOUR LIFE TO JESUS TODAY! AND IF YOU ALREADY HAVE, LIVE FOR HIM, REMEMBER WITHOUT HOLINESS NO MAN WILL SEE THE LORD!!!

Culled from The Word for Today by Bob and Debby Gass with Ruth Gass Halliday, page iv, February-March-April 2017 Edition.

Note: Keep meditating on these insights throughout this week and prayerfully apply them to relevant areas of your life and even those of others.

Prayer Focus: Say these prayers for each day as you meditate on the insights received.

Day 1: Father, by Your grace, please save sinners all over the world.

Day 2: I break the power of Satan and sin over the members of my family in Jesus' Name.

Day 3: Father, please keep me in Your love.

Day 4: I destroy every yoke of untimely death in my family in Jesus' Name.

Day 5: I refuse to be lost in eternity. Lord Jesus, please help me home.

Day 6: Father, please restore all backsliders to their first love.

Day 7: Heavenly Father, let Your Kingdom come.

Week Twenty-Three

Study Focus: Your Light Is Desperately Needed Now
Scriptural Text: Isaiah 60:1-3

Insights for Meditation and Prayerful Application

Beloved, did you know that as at today there are still many people in several places living in darkness? I mean gross darkness as Isaiah 60:2 calls it. And a dictionary has defined darkness to be a lack of knowledge and enlightenment.

Some of these people still live in the darkness of sin because they don't have a working knowledge of God's saving grace; some still live in the darkness of sickness tending towards death because they have not been told of the healing power in the Name of Jesus; some still bow down to false gods because they have not come to know the way to worship the God of Heaven. All these are works of darkness with which the devil has kept them in bondage. You don't need to travel far to notice this trend; they are all around us. And that is exactly why this clarion call is being made at this time. You are being called upon at this critical time to ARISE AND SHINE YOUR LIGHT. The Lord saved your soul not just to sit down in church and feel good, but to reach out to others in need of the kind of light you are enjoying. **The only cure to darkness is light** and the Lord said YOU ARE THE LIGHT OF THE WORLD (Matt 5:14). So, if these people are ever going to be free from the works of darkness, you will necessarily have to shine your light.

The best thing you can do to appreciate God for saving your soul is to TELL OTHERS ABOUT HIM. Remember, it is **DESPERATELY** needed now. Arise and Shine your Light!

Note: Keep meditating on these insights throughout this week and prayerfully apply them to relevant areas of your life and even those of others.

Prayer Focus: Say these prayers for each day as you meditate on the insights received.

Day 1: Father, please destroy every work of darkness in Your church in Jesus' Name.

Day 2: Father, please send more laborers to Your end time harvest of souls.

Day 3: Father, please take away every form of distraction from Your ministers' lives.

Day 4: Father, let Your love draw sinners to Your Kingdom. Save and deliver them.

Day 5: Father, prosper all genuine missions work globally. Let there be good fruits.

Day 6: Father, empower all Your ministers globally for greater harvest of souls.

Day 7: I receive grace to begin to shine my light everywhere I go in Jesus' Name.

Week Twenty-Four

Study Focus: The Mystery of the Holy Communion
Scriptural Text: I Corinthians 11:23-26

<u>Insights for Meditation and Prayerful Application</u>
As you read this, you most probably have partaken in the Holy Communion (the Lord's Supper) at one time or the other. But as I was meditating on what to share with you, it was laid on my heart to show you this brief but life-transforming mystery about the Holy Communion. Firstly, it should be noted that it is not just a church doctrine. The Lord Jesus Himself instituted it before His departure and instructed us to continue in it as a way of remembering Him (1 Corinthians 11:23-26). And take note also that He called it "supper" not breakfast or lunch. He took it at night and asked us to do same.

But aside these, we actually partake of His Body and Blood at the Communion table which implies Covenant Reinforcement. Taking the wine as the representation of His Blood simply means GETTING THE VERY LIFE OF CHRIST (THE SUM TOTAL OF DIVINITY –Colossians 1:19; 2:9) INTO OURSELVES. Because according to Leviticus 17:11, THE LIFE OF THE FLESH IS IN THE BLOOD. You know what that means? By taking the Holy Communion correctly (1Corinthians 11:27-34) and in faith (Rom 14:23), whatever cannot survive in Christ's Blood cannot survive in your body (including all forms of sicknesses and diseases). It also means you can be empowered to live the very life of Christ (with ability to stay free from sin) right here on earth. And what more, your eternity with Jesus can be secured on the platter of

Holy Communion (John 6:53-54). All these, just by partaking in the Holy Communion worthily and with understanding.

The next time you have the opportunity to approach the Lord's Table, have a different mindset and your experience will be different. Trust you are blessed. Please share with others so as to stop missing this blessing. Unbelievers can't partake of Christ's Body and Blood. It's for us; let's GRAB THE OPPORTUNITY!

Note: Keep meditating on these insights throughout this week and prayerfully apply them to relevant areas of your life and even those of others.

Prayer Focus: Say these prayers for each day as you meditate on the insights received.

Day 1: Father, thank You for the gift of Your Son, Jesus Christ.

Day 2: Lord Jesus, thanks for shedding Your Blood for my sins.

Day 3: I receive grace to begin to partake of Your body and blood worthily from now on.

Day 4: Father, please fill my life with all the benefits of the Holy Communion.

Day 5: Father, by the power of this Communion, take away sicknesses from my life.

Day 6: Father, please purify me. Deliver me totally from the power of sin.

Day 7: Lord Jesus, please keep me in Your love till I see Your face in glory.

Week Twenty-Five

Study Focus: Revelation Knowledge Part 1
Scriptural Text: Matthew 4:1-11

<u>Insights for Meditation and Prayerful Application</u>
Note -To get the revelation, you will have to read all and then ACT immediately.
This is a popular portion of the scriptures which talks about the temptation of our Lord Jesus Christ after His 40 days fasting and prayer. Though there are many lessons the Lord has taught and can still teach us from this experience of Jesus with Satan, there is this particular one He has put in my heart to share with you this week.

If you take time to read from verse one to eleven, you will notice that the temptations were actually three (3) in number. The devil presented the first one to Jesus, but He (Jesus) responded by quoting the Word back to him (Satan); the second temptation followed the same trend and even the third. However, if you pay attention to the response of Jesus to the devil upon presenting the third one, you will notice He said something He didn't say during the first and the second. Jesus said in verse 10 *"...Begone, Satan..." (AMP, RSV)*, *"...Away with you, Satan..." (NKJV)*, *"...Beat it, Satan..." (MSG)*, *"...Away from me, Satan..." (NIV)*, *"...Get out of here, Satan..." (TLB, NLT)*, *"...Go away, Satan..." (HCSB, GNT)*, *"...Get thee hence, Satan..." (KJV, AKJV)*, *"...Go, Satan..." (NASB)*, *"...Get behind me, Satan..." (WEB)*, *"...Go away from me, Satan..." (NCV)*.

And what did the devil do? He simply departed (left Him, went away from Him, stopped disturbing Him) just as Jesus demanded (verse 11).

However, note that the devil did not leave until He was told to leave; that was what Eve did not do in the Garden of Eden. The moment Jesus said "Get out of here, Satan", he simply got out and there was no 4th temptation. It ended right there.

James 4: 7 says once you have submitted yourself to God, you are to resist (stop, prevent, hinder) the devil, (not discuss, negotiate, pray about or even cry about the devil). It is only then he will flee from you like he departed from Jesus. If you can live by this principle, I guarantee the devil will never mess around with you again. If you feel any symptom of sickness or disease in your body, don't cry. Simply command like Jesus, "Away from my body, Satan". If your child is misbehaving and all effort to help him has failed, simply resist the devil by saying "Get out of my child's life and affairs, Satan". Make sure you say it like Jesus did. Don't just say "get out", but "get out, Satan" so that he will know he's the one you are talking to. But if you are not yet born again, it can't work. He will just laugh at you. So to live this way, YOU MUST BE BORN AGAIN. And this is the beauty of the whole thing; the moment you ask the devil to leave and he leaves, angels will come and minister to you, helping you to overcome the challenge at hand (Matthew 4:11). Trust you are blessed. Say **"Thank You Jesus for the revelation of Your Word"**.

Note: Keep meditating on these insights throughout this week and prayerfully apply them to relevant areas of your life and even those of others.

Prayer Focus: Say these prayers for each day as you meditate on the insights received.
Day 1: In the Name of Jesus, begone from my health, Satan.
Day 2: In the Name of Jesus, away from my finances, Satan.
Day 3: In the Name of Jesus, go away from my family, Satan.
Day 4: In the Name of Jesus, get out of my ministry, Satan.
Day 5: In the Name of Jesus, get behind my destiny, Satan.
Day 6: In the Name of Jesus, away with you, Satan.
Day 7: In the Name of Jesus, away from me, Satan.

Week Twenty-Six

Study Focus: Revelation Knowledge Part 2
Scriptural Text: Revelation 4:1-11

<u>Insights for Meditation and Prayerful Application</u>
Note -To get the revelation, you will have to read all and then ACT immediately.
John the Revelator was one man the Lord granted unusual revelations, most of which concerns things that are yet to occur but must surely occur. In one of such encounters, he was invited to heaven to witness the way worship and praises are being offered to the Almighty God Who lives forever more (verse 2). According to him, he saw twenty-four elders sitting on twenty-four thrones, clothed in white robes with crowns of gold on their heads falling down before the One Who lives forever more in worship and adoration (verses 4, 10 and 11). But he saw some other **four creatures in heaven which were full of eyes in front, at the back, around and within** worshiping the Lord day and night without resting from eternity past to eternity to come (verse 6-9). At this point I became interested and I asked the Lord why those four creatures who always offer Him praise and worship day and night were not full of noses, ears, mouths or other organs all over their bodies but eyes. **Why eyes in front, at the back, around and within I asked Him?** And in His Wisdom, He responded by saying that is the heavenly pattern of worship and praise typified for men on earth to emulate. He said being full of eyes means "No matter where you are, who you are and what you are experiencing; if you look ahead of you (in the front), you will **see** reasons to praise Me; if you look at your past (at the back), you will **see** reasons to praise Me; if you look around you, you will **see** reasons to praise

Me; and if you look within you, you will **see** reasons to praise Me. So wherever you look, you will clearly see why I should be praised from eternity to eternity. Those creatures are seeing my Hands in the past, my operations now and even my glorious plans for the future and they just can't stop praising Me. **That is my expectation from my children on earth**".

Please dear reader, before you voice out your next complaint, kindly look at what God has seen you through all your life, think about those who are being daily reported dead all around you, look within you and see how God is coordinating your digestive, circulatory and respiratory systems, then look at the beautiful future He has promised you and knowing fully well that He cannot lie (Numbers 23:19); you will naturally overflow in praises. May the Lord grant your eyes the ability to see His goodness in your life. Go ahead and praise Him now, He is waiting to enjoy your praises.

Note: Keep meditating on these insights throughout this week and prayerfully apply them to relevant areas of your life and even those of others.

Prayer Focus: Say these prayers for each day as you meditate on the insights received.
Day 1: Father, thank You for all You have done in my life (mention them).
Day 2: Father, thank You for all You are doing in my life (mention them).
Day 3: Father, thank You for all You will do in my life (declare your expectations).
Day 4: Father, I worship You for Who You are and for all You can do.
Day 5: Father, I worship You for Your wonderful works of creation.
Day 6: Father, I praise You for Your awesome power (sing to Him).
Day 7: Just go ahead and worship the Lord in songs, word, thanks etc.

Week Twenty-Seven

Study Focus: His Witnesses Part 1
Scriptural Text: Acts 1:8

Insights for Meditation and Prayerful Application
The Lord Jesus said His followers (believers) would be **His witnesses** from their immediate environment to the uttermost part of the earth – all by the ability and power the Holy Spirit supplies (Acts 1:8). Though that doesn't sound like a difficult task, yet many of us believers are finding it difficult to carry out partly due to the kind of teachings/methods we have been previously exposed to. Some of us have been taught that in order to evangelize, we must load up our heads with many Bible verses; go from house to house knocking on peoples' doors or preach so convincingly in order to win someone over.
Well, there is nothing wrong in doing any of those things; but my Master said you shall be His witnesses.

Who then is a witness? *A witness is one who gives a testimony based on what he/she has experienced or knows about a person or an event.* Acts 22:15 says *"For thou shall be His witness unto all men of what thou hast seen and heard"*. To evangelize then simply means telling all men that Jesus is the Way to the Father and that He is the ONLY Saviour from sin and eternal death (John 14:6). You are also to support this claim by telling them what you have seen and heard about Jesus. At least you have heard that He heals all sicknesses, He forgives sins, He delivers from all kinds of oppression or you most probably have seen some of His Mighty works in your own very life. Those are the things He wants you to tell others. You don't have to convince anybody. When a witness is called into the box in a law court, he is only asked to say all he knows about the case at hand. Nobody ever asks a witness to convince the court whether a case is true or false. Convincing is the work of the lawyer and Jesus is our Mediator and Advocate Who does the convincing through His Holy Spirit (1 John 2:1, John 16:13).

However, note that the Master only said "Go ye..." in the Great Commission according to Matthew 28:18-20; He didn't specify "How" you are to go. This will be considered in the Part 2 of this piece. Once you are saved, you have a standing order to tell others about the One Who saved you. Arise and get into the witnessing business, the reward is so handsome. Shalom!

Note: Keep meditating on these insights throughout this week and prayerfully apply them to relevant areas of your life and even those of others.

Prayer Focus: Say these prayers for each day as you meditate on the insights received.
Day 1: Father, I thank You for the Good News of Your Son Jesus Christ.
Day 2: Father, let Your Resurrection power become evident in every aspect of my life.
Day 3: Father, please empower me to know You more.
Day 4: Father, please let Your grace that brings salvation appear to all sinners globally.
Day 5: Heavenly Father, please make me a worthy witness to Your Son Jesus Christ.
Day 6: Father, please let my life be a testimony of Your goodness and mercies.
Day 7: Father, let me never bring You shame all the days of my life.

Week Twenty-Eight

Study Focus: His Witnesses Part 2
Scriptural Text: Matthew 28:18-20

Insights for Meditation and Prayerful Application

Beloved, we heartily rejoice with you for the privilege of experiencing another beautiful week in the land of the living. From our last ministration titled "His Witnesses Part 1", we discovered that the Lord Jesus Christ only wants us as believers to be His witnesses to the whole world of the things which we have seen and heard about Him by the power of the Holy Spirit (Acts 1:8, Acts 22:15). And that is to continue until the whole world is reached and then the end will come (Matt 24:14).

Now, how are we to go about this? It's very simple. Get baptized in the Holy Ghost (Luke 11:13) and "Go ye into the world" with the gospel as Christ's witness by doing any of the following:

- **Write it** – as tracts, books, pamphlets, letters, bulletins, cards etc
- **Wear it** – print the message on shirts, caps, tags, wrist bands, and wear them. Also print on windscreens, doorposts etc
- **Share it** – in meetings, discussions, trainings, workshops etc
- **Air it** – on Radios, Television, Cable Channels etc
- **Post it** – on facebook, twitter, instagram, blogsites, and on the internet generally.
- **Drive/Sponsor it** – form an evangelical group, join an existing group, promote or fund the activities of soul winners' group (missions).

- **Sing it** – compose songs, wax albums, do soundtracks, caller-tunes etc
- **Organize/Arrange it** – through luncheons, tourism, cruises, trips, parties, seminars etc
- **Act it** – through drama, road shows, film shows, cinemas etc
- **Pray it** – by interceding for sinners' salvation, asking God to send more laborers into His harvest (Matt 9:37-38)
- **Live it** – by your lifestyle, dispositions, behavior (Acts 11:26; 4:13)
- **Preach it** – verbally either publicly or privately, in houses, streets, shops. Also to individuals or groups of people.

By all means, just keep witnessing.
JESUS IS THE BEST PRODUCT ANYONE CAN MARKET!
Reward: Everything you need and will ever need in life is guaranteed once you become His witness – Matthew 6:33.

Note: Keep meditating on these insights throughout this week and prayerfully apply them to relevant areas of your life and even those of others.

Prayer Focus: Say these prayers for each day as you meditate on the insights received.
Day 1: Father, thank You for the Great Commission to reach the world for You.
Day 2: Father, release the power to be an effective witness upon me.
Day 3: Father, I receive the grace to preach and teach Your Word everywhere I go.
Day 4: Father, please let my life draw countless souls to Your Kingdom.
Day 5: Father, please help me to use all my gifts to bring profits to Your Kingdom.
Day 6: Father, turn all my weaknesses to strength and use me for Your glory.
Day 7: Father, please let thy Kingdom come upon the earth.

Week Twenty-Nine

Study Focus: Have You Insured Your Life?
Scriptural Text: Psalm 121:3-8

Insights for Meditation and Prayerful Application

Assurance of salvation is the only channel through which you can access a life insurance in Jesus Christ. There is no other way you can insure your life except in the Lord Jesus our Savior. Only Jesus can give a guaranteed life insurance.

When your life is insured in Jesus, you have guaranteed security in this world which is full of daily cases of crises and terrorism (Psalm 121: 3-8). Little wonder the scripture says Christ in you is the hope of glory (Colossians 1: 27b). That is, Christ is the hope of eternal life; the evidence, the license, the access, the receipt, the password, the secret code, the channel, the route, the gateway to a glorious life, not only in heaven but also here on earth.

Only Jesus can give you assurance of peace in the midst of troubles and storms of life; divine health in the presence of endemic/epidemic outbreak of diseases; true prosperity in the midst of lack and insufficiency; divine favor where you were once despised; breakthrough in the midst of difficulties; a life of dominion over this world and its negative influence. In actual fact, you can be like *a tree planted by the rivers of water that bringeth forth its fruits in season* (Psalm 1: 3).

The reverse becomes the case when Jesus is absent in your life, verse 4 of the same scripture says: *the ungodly are not so but are like the chaff which the wind driveth away.*

If you must experience the life of abundance with peace on every side, you need Jesus (Phil 4:19).

Every good thing is embedded in Jesus, eternal life inclusive. So make a choice today.

If you really need Jesus to step into your life and situation, it can happen right now. Just say the prayer below with faith in your heart:

"Dear Lord, I know you died for me and I am very sorry for all the wrong things I have done. I acknowledge you as my Lord and Savior. Please come into my life and take your place; take control of my life completely henceforth in Jesus' Name. Amen".

Congrats!

You have just acquired a life insurance with no expiry date. Enjoy your insurance!

Note: Keep meditating on these insights throughout this week and prayerfully apply them to relevant areas of your life and even those of others.

Prayer Focus: Say these prayers for each day as you meditate on the insights received.

Day 1: Blood of Jesus, avail for me and all my family members today.

Day 2: I pray for divine insurance of all that are precious to me in Jesus' Name.

Day 3: Father, please save all my unsaved relatives by Your grace today.

Day 4: I break the power of Satan and sin over all my family members in Jesus' Name.

Day 5: Satan, my life is insured in Christ. So, you have no part in me in Jesus' Name.

Day 6: I declare by the power in the Name of Jesus, sin shall no longer dominate me.

Day 7: I secure my eternity in Heaven by the Blood of Jesus. Amen.

Week Thirty

Study Focus: Handling Moments of Attack
Scriptural Text: Matthew 26:41

<u>Insights for Meditation and Prayerful Application</u>
There is a popular hymn titled "Christian, seek not yet repose". The first stanza reads:
Christian, seek not yet repose;
Hear thy guardian angel say,
"Thou art in the midst of foes:
Watch and pray!"
You may want to see the other stanzas for better understanding of the message.
As a believer, you are branded for Christ in the spirit realm. As a matter of fact, you are on uniform the same way earthly soldiers wear theirs. Your earthly neighbours may not know you are a Christian but the devil knows as well as his ever active demons.
Please beware of these seasons in your life because the devil leverages on them to strike:
Immediately after a breakthrough (promotion, testimony, marriage, safe delivery, answered prayers etc);
Moments of disappointment, discouragement and despondency;
Immediately after a major divine revelation [Matthew 3:16-17; 4:1-3; 16:16-19, 21-23]; and other seasons of vulnerability when your guards are down.

The devil is wise enough to stay away from you when you are so spiritually high and hot. He knows when you become unsuspecting and he launches his attacks at such moments.

What then is the way out? – **Watch and Pray** [Matthew 26:41]. Not just 'Pray' please, but 'Watch and Pray!' **Praying** without **watching** is what has made Christians objects of ridicule in the hands of their chief adversary - the devil.

Once again, Watch and Pray!

God bless You.

Note: Keep meditating on these insights throughout this week and prayerfully apply them to relevant areas of your life and even those of others.

Prayer Focus: Say these prayers for each day as you meditate on the insights received.

Day 1: I refuse to become a victim of satanic attack in Jesus' Name.

Day 2: I am more than conquerors through Christ's love for me. I will not fall.

Day 3: Father, please guard me with strength in my inner man when I am weak and down.

Day 4: Father, please do not give me over to the will of my adversaries.

Day 5: Every trap the devil has set for me and my family, we escape all in Jesus' Name.

Day 6: I receive the grace to be watchful and prayerful in the Name of Jesus.

Day 7: Father, please turn all my seen and unseen foes to my footstool in Jesus' Name.

Week Thirty-One

Study Focus: You Own Nothing
Scriptural Text: 2 Corinthians 6:10c

Insights for Meditation and Prayerful Application
As a Christian, you really own nothing. Whatever the Lord gives you or releases in your direction belongs to Him. He only gives them to you to enjoy. 1 Corinthians 10:26 says '...the earth and every good thing in it belongs to the Lord and is yours to enjoy'. That shows God alone is the owner of all things; man only possesses them at one time or the other. This mindset should help you never to hold on too tightly to anything you possess here on earth. If God (the Owner of all things) decides to ask you for any of the things He has given you to enjoy, you are expected to quickly give it to Him, and even appreciate Him for allowing you to enjoy it in the first place. John 3:27 says a man has nothing except he be given from above. Job 1:21 also confirms this.

Action: Don't hold on to anything; only enjoy it with a sense of gratitude to the Owner. Never forget that!

Note: Keep meditating on these insights throughout this week and prayerfully apply them to relevant areas of your life and even those of others.

Prayer Focus: Say these prayers for each day as you meditate on the insights received.
Day 1: Father, thank You for giving me all things to enjoy.

Day 2: Father, please restore to me every good thing that has been stolen from me.

Day 3: I cover all my blessings and testimonies in the Blood of Jesus.

Day 4: Father, please open my eyes and lead me to where my blessings are.

Day 5: Father, please cut off the hands of the adversary in my family and ministry.

Day 6: Lord Jesus, I receive the grace to walk in Your love, truth and knowledge.

Day 7: Father, I am grateful for all You are still going to give to me in this life and beyond.

Week Thirty-Two

Study Focus: Do You Also Hate Them?
Scriptural Text: Proverbs 6:16-19

Insights for Meditation and Prayerful Application

Proverbs 6:16-19 (AMP) presents a list of 7 things which the Lord hates; and as a child of God, not only should they not be found in your life, you must also hate them. They are:

- A proud look (the spirit that makes one overestimate himself and underestimate others)
- A lying tongue
- Hands that shed innocent blood
- A heart that manufactures wicked thoughts and plans
- Feet that are swift in running to evil
- A false witness who breathes out lies (even under oath)
- He who sows discord among his brethren

Run a thorough scan on your life; if you discover any of these, quickly ask the Lord for help in order to be free from them. Why? It is simply because THE LORD HATES THEM!

Note: Keep meditating on these insights throughout this week and prayerfully apply them to relevant areas of your life and even those of others.

Prayer Focus: Say these prayers for each day as you meditate on the insights received.

Day 1: Father, please completely deliver me from a proud look and haughty spirit.

Day 2: Father, please give me total victory over lies of all kinds. Purify my tongue.

Day 3: Father, please keep my hands from shedding innocent blood.

Day 4: Father, please fill my heart with Your own godly thoughts and plans.

Day 5: Father, please keep my feet from running to evil. Order my steps in Your Word.

Day 6: Father, please deliver me from lying witnesses and keep me from becoming one.

Day 7: Father, please keep me from sowing discord among brethren. Help me Lord.

Week Thirty-Three

Study Focus: Thoughts on Gratitude
Scriptural Text: I Thessalonians 5:18

Insights for Meditation and Prayerful Application
Why should we be grateful?

1. **The Lord expects it** – in Luke 17:17-18, the Lord waited patiently to receive the cured lepers' gratitude. He still expects same from us today.
2. **We only know in part** – 1 Corinthians 13:9a says we don't always know the whole story. So even if events don't turn out as expected, because of the part we don't know but which the Lord knows, we must be grateful.
3. **It is God's will** – 1 Thessalonians 5:18 and Romans 8:28 portray gratitude as God's will. Meaning, not being grateful is contrary to His will. Moreover, everything that happens to us has one ultimate goal as far as God is concerned - they are working together for our good. That should make us grateful.

What if we refuse to be grateful?
Please read **Psalm 28:5** for the answer. You won't like to experience that.
Watch Out: Every time you are complaining, grumbling, nagging or murmuring about anything, you are not practicing gratitude. You can't be murmuring and be grateful at the same time.
Receive grace to be grateful henceforth in Jesus' Name.
Shalom!!!

Note: Keep meditating on these insights throughout this week and prayerfully apply them to relevant areas of your life and even those of others.

Prayer Focus: Say these prayers for each day as you meditate on the insights received.

Day 1: Heavenly Father, please fill my heart with the attitude of gratitude.

Day 2: Father, thank You for all Your goodness towards me and my family.

Day 3: Father, thank You for the occurrences in my life to which I have no explanation.

Day 4: Father, I thank You because indeed all things work together for my good.

Day 5: Father, I rejoice in all the benefits You have caused me to enjoy so far.

Day 6: Father, I thank You for the beautiful future You have prepared for me.

Day 7: Father, please totally deliver me from complaining, murmuring and grumbling.

Week Thirty-Four

Study Focus: Forgiveness Made Easy
Scriptural Text: Ephesians 4:32

<u>**Insights for Meditation and Prayerful Application**</u>
Is it really possible to live in this world without being offended by anyone? I believe the honest and sincere answer to that is 'No'. However, there is this thing the Lord expects of everyone who gets offended, and that is forgiveness. Well, this may sound like what someone may not want to hear because it sometimes seems difficult to forgive especially when one is deeply hurt. But to God be the glory, there is a way out. Ephesians 4:32 says 'And be ye kind one to another, tenderhearted, **forgiving one another, even as God for Christ's sake hath forgiven you**' (emphasis mine). That's it. God forgave and still forgives our sins not because we deserve to be forgiven but because of Christ's sacrifice for us. And the Lord expects us to do same. To find it easy to forgive your offenders, stop focusing on the offence or the offender. Focus on Christ's love for the world (which includes your offender), and just go ahead and forgive **for Christ's sake**. Now, they may not deserve your forgiveness but for Christ's sake, they must still be forgiven.

Also, not forgiving your offenders makes you a prison warder whose job is to ensure the prisoners do not escape and as such becomes imprisoned as well. Get this; **your offender needs your forgiveness more than you need his/her apology**. Your freedom depends on his release. Receive grace to let go in Jesus name.
Shalom!!!

Note: Keep meditating on these insights throughout this week and prayerfully apply them to relevant areas of your life and even those of others.

Prayer Focus: Say these prayers for each day as you meditate on the insights received.

Day 1: Father, I thank You for the forgiveness I have received for all my sins.

Day 2: I receive the grace to forgive all my offenders in Jesus' Name.

Day 3: Father, please grant me the grace to be kind and tenderhearted towards others.

Day 4: I release all my offenders for Christ's sake. I let them go in Jesus' Name.

Day 5: Father, please teach me how to overlook insults and offences like Jesus.

Day 6: Father, please let me be like You in love and mercy.

Day 7: Every good thing unforgiving spirit has taken away from my life is restored now.

Week Thirty-Five

Study Focus: Who Touched Me?
Scriptural Text: Luke 8:46

<u>**Insights for Meditation and Prayerful Application**</u>
Luke 8:46 [AKJV] says 'And Jesus said, somebody hath touched me; for I perceive that virtue is gone out of me'.
What is the implication of this? It means whenever a man touches God, virtues are released in his direction". When you touch Him, you receive your desired (purposed and expected) miracle(s).
Analyzing this statement also reveals something else. Jesus said 'somebody hath touched me' –not an Apostle, Prophet, Evangelist, Pastor, Deacon or Deaconess – hath touched me. He said 'somebody'; and somebody could actually be anybody. This means you don't need a spiritual pedigree or church title to be able or to qualify to touch Jesus. Anyone who can find their way to Jesus can touch Him – He is no respecter of persons (Rom 2:11; 1 Peter 1:17).

In our text, so many apostles and disciples had contact with Jesus, but it was only a stinking, despised and afflicted woman with 12years issue of blood who really TOUCHED Him (by her faith). And that means you too can touch Him –Praise God!

Note: Keep meditating on these insights throughout this week and prayerfully apply them to relevant areas of your life and even those of others.

Prayer Focus: Say these prayers for each day as you meditate on the insights received.

Day 1: Father, I bless You for Your miracle working power displayed through Your Son.

Day 2: Father, please deliver me from every form of unbelief.

Day 3: Father, please help my faith. Help me grow in Your knowledge.

Day 4: I touch Jesus by faith today and all issues in my life become resolved now.

Day 5: I release my faith today, every long-standing problem in my family is over now.

Day 6: Lord Jesus, please cause Your virtue to flow into every area of my life from today.

Day 7: Father as I walk according to Your Word, please daily honor my faith.

Week Thirty-Six

Study Focus: It's Not Yet a Sacrifice until It Bleeds
Scriptural Text: John 3:16-18

<u>**Insights for Meditation and Prayerful Application**</u>
This is a very short and precise revelation. Read and meditate on it, it will change something in you.
"The more the pain your giving generates in your heart, the more the joy in the heart of the recipient. And the more the joy in the heart of the recipient, the more the God of harvest gets involved in eradicating every other form of pain in your life".
Beloved, don't just give; give painfully and sacrificially. Your giving should cost you something precious (2 Samuel 24:24). This is the kind of giving God Himself demonstrated in John 3:16 when He gave all He had for the redemption of worthless and unpromising sinners; and He expects same from you. In Genesis 4:3-7 two brothers - Cain and Abel - offered unto the Lord; but it was Abel's offering that God commended while He condemned Cain's. Why? Abel offered the firstling – the choicest part - of his flock while Cain offered some of his produce. Abel offered sacrificially but Cain offered conveniently and God noticed that. Let your offering reflect the VALUE you place on God (Who actually is the Giver of all things including the things you are to offer unto Him). Meditate on this and act accordingly, you are next in line for a bountiful harvest.
Remember, it's not yet a sacrifice until it bleeds.

Note: Keep meditating on these insights throughout this week and prayerfully apply them to relevant areas of your life and even those of others.

Prayer Focus: Say these prayers for each day as you meditate on the insights received.

Day 1: Lord, I thank You for sending Your Son to die for me, my family and friends.

Day 2: Father, bless me always that I might be a blessing to others at all times.

Day 3: Grace to give rightly at all times please release upon me in Jesus' Name.

Day 4: Father, please let not the death of Your Son Jesus be in vain over my life.

Day 5: Father, let the due harvests on my giving manifest in Jesus' Name.

Day 6: Lord Jesus, make me a continuous source of blessing to people around me.

Day 7: Father, help me to always give sacrificially like You. Let me always glorify You.

Week Thirty-Seven

Study Focus: The Truth about Lies [Part 1]
Scriptural Text: Proverbs 12:19

Insights for Meditation and Prayerful Application
Proverbs 12:19 (GNT) says 'Lies have a short life but truth lives on forever'
If lies have a short life, what legal or moral justification do liars have to expect to live long? In case you are wondering if you are a liar, let me help you. A dictionary has described a lie to be a false statement made deliberately in order to deceive; an intentional untruth...
To be a liar, all you need do is say or do something that is not the truth deliberately... And a lie is a lie, no types or colours. Think about this please. We will continue from here next week God willing. God bless you mightily!

Note: Keep meditating on these insights throughout this week and prayerfully apply them to relevant areas of your life and even those of others.

Prayer Focus: Say these prayers for each day as you meditate on the insights received.
Day 1: Lord I thank You for the Truth in Your Word.
Day 2: Lord, please reveal areas of my life where I need to make amends about lying.
Day 3: Lord Jesus, please help me to say the truth always.
Day 4: Father, replace every lie of the devil I have believed over my life with Your truth.

Day 5: Lord please restore to me every blessing lies have robbed me of in Jesus' Name.

Day 6: Lord Jesus, give me the grace to share Your truth with people everywhere I go.

Day 7: Help me Lord to live a long and fulfilled life in Jesus Name.

Week Thirty-Eight

Study Focus: The Truth about Lies [Part 2]
Scriptural Text: Proverbs 6:16-19

Insights for Meditation and Prayerful Application

Proverbs 6:16-19 present a list of seven things the Lord hates, and lies just happened to appear twice in that list. It is against this background that we decided to study this thing called 'lie' especially in order to discover how we can avoid it since the Lord Himself hates it.

From last week's message, a lie was described as a false statement made with deliberate intent to deceive. From this definition, some facts become vivid;

Anything that is false qualifies as a lie.

To lie is a deliberate action. You can't say "I didn't know I lied". It is different from 'a slip of tongue'. Lying is an intentional act.

The purpose or aim of every lie is to deceive – to make one believe the opposite of the truth. To make one take as true what actually is false. And deceit as defined by a dictionary is the practice of deceiving; concealment or distortion of the truth for the purpose of misleading. So, to deceive is to mislead one from the truth either by totally concealing it or distorting it.

Now pause for a while and meditatively look at your life. Then, honestly answer this question: **Am I a liar?**

Note: Keep meditating on these insights throughout this week and prayerfully apply them to relevant areas of your life and even those of others.

Prayer Focus: Say these prayers for each day as you meditate on the insights received.

Day 1: Lord, help me to detest lie the way You do in Jesus Name.

Day 2: Every lie I have ever told, please Lord forgive me.

Day 3: In every area I have misled people due to lies please have mercy on me.

Day 4: Help me Lord to always profess Your truth.

Day 5: Lord Jesus, help me to be a true witness always.

Day 6: Satan, I reject all your lies over my life and family in Jesus' Name.

Day 7: Spirit of Truth, please take me over completely.

Week Thirty-Nine

Study Focus: The Truth about Lies [Part 3]
Scriptural Text: Proverbs 12:19

<u>**Insights for Meditation and Prayerful Application**</u>
From our discussion last week, we can simply infer that whoever tells a lie is not unaware of the truth. That is, every liar knows the truth. They are not liars because they don't know the truth; they just choose not to work with it. So, a liar is actually one who deliberately presents the opposite of the truth even when he knows the truth.

Today, we want to look at avenues through which lies find expression in our lives. This is not to judge you but to draw your attention to something you might not be taking note of.

Through our words (verbal lies) – e.g "When did you resume at work today?" At 7:30am sir. And you know you resumed at 8:45am.

Through our writings (written lies) – e.g "How much did you buy the gas? Please include it in your report". And you write 3, 500NGN when it was actually 1, 500NGN.

Through our online chatting like on WhatsApp, Messenger, Instagram, Facebook, E-mail etc (Electronic lies or e-lies) – e.g "Baby, where are you now?" And you respond to the chat by typing "I am at Shoprite now" when in actual fact you are planning to wash your clothes at home.

Through your appearance in dressing and carriage (cosmetic lies or imposture) – e.g by pretending to be who you are not just to impress or gain undue advantage over an unsuspecting person.

Through other means such as deceptive actions, looks, gesticulations, presentation of fake certificates etc. As a matter of fact, anything that is false (not true) is a lie.

If you have been involved in any of these, please repent and stop it before it is too late. God is willing to forgive you and give you a new beginning. Remember, there is still a solid relationship between "lies" and "untimely death" – Psalm 55:23, Psalm 63:11.
Shalom!

Note: Keep meditating on these insights throughout this week and prayerfully apply them to relevant areas of your life and even those of others.

Prayer Focus: Say these prayers for each day as you meditate on the insights received.
Day 1: Lord Jesus I thank You for this new week.
Day 2: Father, thank You for the eye opening teachings for these past weeks.
Day 3: Lord, please forgive me for every verbal lies I have committed.
Day 4: Lord, please forgive me for every written lies I have committed.
Day 5: Lord, please forgive me for every electronic/online lies I have committed.
Day 6: Lord Jesus please give me a new beginning in Your truth.
Day 7: Lord, let Your truth abide in my heart forever.

Week Forty

Study Focus: The Truth about Lies [Part 4]
Scriptural Text: Proverbs 12:19

<u>**Insights for Meditation and Prayerful Application**</u>
Whao! It's another beautiful week; and may the joy of the Lord remain upon us all in Jesus' Name.
This week we shall be concluding our study on the subject of 'lies' – having considered it for some weeks now. The text we have been considering is Proverbs 12:19 (GNT) which says 'A lie has a short life, but truth lives on forever'. Before we look at the 'truth' part of this scripture, let us take note of this additional fact about 'lies' – the devil is the father of all lies and liars (John 8:44). The Lord Jesus said there is no truth in him; and the Book of Revelation describes him as one who deceives the whole world. Therefore all his activities are lies, all liars are his children and he together with his lies and liars has a short life (Revelation 12:12; 21:8).

Now, the truth is that which is true (genuine, exact, real, authentic, reliable, unfailing, sure etc). And believe me; no other adjective can better describe the Word of God (the Bible) than this definition. God is the Source of truth, and knowing Him is what guarantees total freedom from all the lies of the devil as well as activities of all liars (John 8:32). As a matter of fact, you can't really be described as truthful without an encounter with the Spirit of Truth.

Failure to activate the Spirit of truth is what perpetuates the activities of the devil (lies) in any life or organization. Speak the truth always, live by the truth always and your freedom will be guaranteed.

Note these:

The reason the Bible says the truth lives on forever is because the Source of all truths (God) lives on forever (Rev 4:9-10).

And the reason the Bible also says lies have a short life is because the source of all lies (Devil) has a short time (Rev 12:12).

THIS MEANS IF YOU LIVE BY THE TRUTH, YOU TOO SHALL LIVE FOREVER (AFTER YOUR LIFE ON THIS EARTH). BUT IF YOU CHOOSE TO CONTINUE IN YOUR LIES, YOU HAVE A SHORT TIME LIKE YOUR FATHER. The choice is yours!

Note: Keep meditating on these insights throughout this week and prayerfully apply them to relevant areas of your life and even those of others.

Prayer Focus: Say these prayers for each day as you meditate on the insights received.

Day 1: Lord, I thank You for this glorious week.

Day 2: Thank You Jesus for the total freedom You have given me over lies.

Day 3: Lord, help me to live by the truth always that I might reign with You forever.

Day 4: Holy Spirit You are the Spirit of Truth. Possess all believers afresh in Jesus Name.

Day 5: Father, please pour out Your Spirit of Truth upon Your Church in these last days.

Day 6: Father, please destroy every work of the devil remaining in my life in Jesus' Name.

Day 7: I receive the grace to daily overcome the temptation to lie in Jesus' Name.

Week Forty-One

Study Focus: A Letter from a Friend to You
Scriptural Text: I Peter 5:7

Insights for Meditation and Prayerful Application
Dear One,
I just had to send a note to tell you how much I love you and care about you.
I saw you yesterday as you were walking and talking with your friends. I waited all day hoping you would want to walk and talk with me also, hoping you'd find time to fellowship with me too, but you didn't.

As evening drew near, I gave you the sunset to close your day and cool breeze to rest you. I waited but you never came. It hurts me so much but I still love you. I always will.
I watched you fall asleep last night and longed to touch you and so slipped the moonlight unto your face. I watched you all night waiting for the morning.
But you awakened late the next day and rushed off to work. You looked so bad, so all alone. It makes my heart ache because I long to help you. I long to reach out to you and comfort you, but will you let Me, will you invite Me? No, you don't have the time.
You shut Me out, battling with your troubles alone. But I love you. I still love you and always will. If only you would listen to me. I really love you. I try to tell you in the blue sky and in the quiet green grass. I whisper in the leaves on the trees and breathe it in the colour of the flowers. I shout it to you from the mountain tops and give the bird songs of love

to sing to you. I clothe you with warm sunshine and perfume the air with natural scents, all for you.

My love for you is deeper than the ocean and bigger than the biggest want or need in your heart. If you only knew how much I want to help you. Just call Me, ask Me, talk to Me - allow Me. I have so many gifts for you. So much I want to share with you.
But I won't hassle you. You are free to call Me. It's up to you. It's your decision.
It's Me, **Jesus Christ** – your Burden Bearer!

Note: Keep meditating on these insights throughout this week and prayerfully apply them to relevant areas of your life and even those of others.

Prayer Focus: Say these prayers for each day as you meditate on the insights received.
Day 1: Dear Lord Jesus, I cast all my burdens on You. Please help me.
Day 2: Father, help me to always put You first in all I do in Jesus' Name.
Day 3: Father, please preserve my going out and coming in today.
Day 4: Father, everywhere I turn today let me meet with Your favor.
Day 5: Heavenly Father, please take away everything distracting me from knowing You.
Day 6: Lord Jesus, please teach me Your ways and direct my paths.
Day 7: Father, please let me never offend You again till I see Your face in glory.

Week Forty-Two

Study Focus: Write Them Down
Scriptural Text: Jeremiah 30:2

<u>**Insights for Meditation and Prayerful Application**</u>
There is something we believers take for granted in relating with God, and it is especially common among Ministers. We go to God in prayers asking Him for revelation or we go into His Word trying to get a message from Him. And when He tells us or shows us something, we just become glad without taking time to write them down. This is one factor responsible for revelation without corresponding action which inevitably culminates in lack of desired results. When God tells you or shows you something, He expects you to get it written (documented). In Jeremiah 30:2 He commanded the Prophet to write all He told him in a book; before He began to show John the Revelator the things to come, He instructed him to write (Revelation 1:19). One of the reasons the Lord doesn't tell or show some of us things is because He knows we won't write them down for necessary action. We just want to feel good with the fact that God speaks to us. There are two main reasons God wants us to write the things He shows or tells us; firstly, He wants to be quoted. That is, He wants to be used as reference (Isaiah 46:9-10, 48:3-8). And this is why we keep seeing "it is written" across the entire scriptures. If they had not been written, there would be no reference.

Secondly, He wants to give the future generations opportunity to walk in the light of His Word. Daniel said he understood by books (as documented by Prophet Jeremiah) that their captivity in Babylon was not to exceed 70 years and he took the necessary steps to obtain his people's freedom (Daniel 9:2-3; Jeremiah 29:4-10). What if Jeremiah had not written, how would Daniel have run with that vital information? Habakkuk 2:2-3 tells of some visions which are meant for the future generations to run with, and it says they are to be written plainly in order for the readers to run with them.

Please learn to write down the things the Lord reveals to you (for your personal use and if applicable, for the general public), it will give you access to more revelation from Him and the purpose of such revelation will not be defeated. Remember, once revealed, they are no longer secrets (Deuteronomy 29:29, Matthew 10:27).

God Bless You!

Note: Keep meditating on these insights throughout this week and prayerfully apply them to relevant areas of your life and even those of others.

Prayer Focus: Say these prayers for each day as you meditate on the insights received.

Day 1: Father, thank You for all the revelations I have received from You.

Day 2: Father, I thank You for Your spirit of understanding at work in me.

Day 3: Father, please increase my level of wisdom in Jesus' Name.

Day 4: Father, please grant me access into more revelations in Jesus' Name.

Day 5: Father, please let me profit from all You have revealed to me.

Day 6: Father, please separate from me every vision/dream killer in Jesus' Name.

Day 7: I receive the grace to daily walk in the light of the Word of God in Jesus' Name.

Week Forty-Three

Study Focus: You Can Win This Battle
Scriptural Text: 1 Samuel 17:32-37, 48-51

<u>**Insights for Meditation and Prayerful Application**</u>
Are you fighting a battle that seems impossible to win? This is what to do. Go back to your previous testimonies. The strength and energy needed to overcome lie therein.
Remember David? He needed the courage and energy to defeat a seemingly insurmountable enemy of the entire nation of Israel – Goliath, and all he did was to call to remembrance how God helped him to destroy the bear and lion that previously attacked him. With that assurance, he simply announced that Goliath (the present battle) will be like one of them (the previous battles). And guess what? That was exactly what happened; he (though a teenager) defeated a well experienced and fully armed giant (Goliath) – 1 Samuel 17:32-37, 48-51.

Do same, the God of David has not changed a bit (Malachi 3:6; Hebrews 13:8).
Praise God!

Note: Keep meditating on these insights throughout this week and prayerfully apply them to relevant areas of your life and even those of others.

Prayer Focus: Say these prayers for each day as you meditate on the insights received.

Day 1: Father, thank You for all the victories You have caused me to enjoy in times past.

Day 2: Father, I give You all the glory for always putting my enemies to shame.

Day 3: Father, thank You for Your spirit of courage and boldness at work in me daily.

Day 4: As I go about today, I declare that I am more than conquerors in Jesus' Name.

Day 5: Powers assigned to frustrate my efforts, be destroyed in the Name of Jesus.

Day 6: Battles transferred to me from my ancestors, end now in the Name of Jesus.

Day 7: From today, I receive victory over every battle that comes my way in Jesus' Name.

Week Forty-Four

Study Focus: There Is A Place
Scriptural Text: Revelation 21:8

Insights for Meditation and Prayerful Application
It is a place of unending tears, crying, sorrow and torment. The occupants of this place groan in regrets because of opportunities they have wasted, the wrong decisions they have made and also the bad choices they have embraced.

In this place, both great and small are subjected to the same treatment of intense pain and agony. As a matter of fact, in this particular place Politicians, Bishops, Pastors, Prostitutes, Armed robbers, Assassins, Civil servants, Presidents of nations, Kings, Messengers etc have the same fate of perpetual suffering.

There is more to this place, none of the occupants has the opportunity to escape the aforementioned experiences; not even through death. It is a cup they must fully drink.
To belong to this place is not difficult at all, you only need to intensify the rate at which you tell lies, cheat, fornicate and gossip. Also, you will need to commit adultery the more as well as idolatry. Just keep living in total disobedience to all God's instructions for living (the Bible), and you will soon join the people there.
However, if your decision is never to find yourself there, you only have one task to carry out. You must URGENTLY REPENT OF ALL YOUR SINS AND CALL ON THE LORD JESUS CHRIST TO SAVE YOUR

SOUL. He is the only Way out of this terrible place. If you follow Him, you will never be lost.

The place is called Hell (eternal damnation). Act Now and Act Fast, people go to Hell daily. Please let others know about this too, it is a place you will not wish for even your enemies.

Note: Keep meditating on these insights throughout this week and prayerfully apply them to relevant areas of your life and even those of others.

Prayer Focus: Say these prayers for each day as you meditate on the insights received.

Day 1: Father, please break the power of Satan and sin over my life in Jesus' Name.

Day 2: Powers dragging my family to hell, loose your hold on them now in Jesus' Name.

Day 3: I refuse to be a victim of hell. Lord Jesus, preserve me by Your grace.

Day 4: I confess all my secret sins to You my Father, please cleanse me totally.

Day 5: Lord Jesus, please deliver my church members from the danger of hell.

Day 6: Father, please purify Your church and deliver her from the gates of hell.

Day 7: Heavenly Father, please let sinners all over the world experience Your salvation.

Week Forty-Five

Study Focus: What Will You Call It?
Scriptural Text: Genesis 2:19

Insights for Meditation and Prayerful Application
In Genesis 2:19, the Lord God created some animals and brought them to Adam to see what he would call them. And it was recorded that whatever Adam called them became their names (without any form of interference from God).
In the same vein, the Lord consciously allows some circumstances to come our way just to see what we will call them. And just as He didn't interfere with Adam's discretion back then, He may not change whatever you call your own.

As a child of God, learn to use the power of your tongue to your own advantage. Don't call that thing troubling your belly stomach ache or fibroid if you are in need of a child, rather call it 'baby is kicking' and it shall be so. You have just received a note from your Landlord and you are panicking because they wrote 'quit notice' on it. Stop panicking, call it 'my letter of promotion to become a Landlord' and you will be surprised at how things will turn out.

Always remember this: There is no situation that has its own name, they only bear the names we give to them. Also note this, "YOUR CONFESSION IN THE TIME OF YOUR CONFUSION IS THE CONCLUSION OF YOUR CONDITION".
Shalom!!!

Note: Keep meditating on these insights throughout this week and prayerfully apply them to relevant areas of your life and even those of others.

Prayer Focus: Say these prayers for each day as you meditate on the insights received.

Day 1: I am blessed beyond every form of embarrassment and shame in Jesus' Name.

Day 2: I am healthy, my family members are healthy and we are serving the Lord.

Day 3: I can't be poor. Through Christ's poverty, I am now rich in all things.

Day 4: I am flying higher than my peers because I am never beneath but above only.

Day 5: I reject every negative suggestions of the devil in Jesus' Name. I am victorious.

Day 6: I reverse every negative trend in my family in Jesus' Name. We are set free.

Day 7: My words will no longer work against me but in my favor in Jesus' Name.

Week Forty-Six

Study Focus: Have You Really Considered This?
Scriptural Text: Colossians 2:9-10

Insights for Meditation and Prayerful Application

I'm not very sure you have really grasped the implication of Colossians 2:9-10 where it says Christ is the Head of all principality and power. Have you? Demonic forces have hierarchies just like human soldiers. They have senior and junior officers, and their tasks are based on their ranks. Among these dark forces, principalities and powers rank as very senior officers. You can confirm this in Ephesians 6:12. They are very wicked. Yet the Word of the Lord says Christ (the One you received at Salvation Who now lives in you) is the Head of ALL PRINCIPALITY AND POWER. This simply means all these forces cannot carry out a single operation anywhere without the knowledge and permission of the Head. He will have to allow them before they can operate anywhere. And if you have surrendered your life to Him (Christ, their Head), you can be sure He will never grant them permission to afflict you.

Running from witches and wizards is a clear sign of insanity if you are in Christ. These are very junior officers in the Kingdom of darkness. They are like messengers with very low ranks. And if principalities and powers (chief officers) shake and tremble before the Head, they dare not near you if you are in Christ. The Lord laid this on my heart to share with you and I have just done so. Please kindly find your place in Christ, understand your privileges and behave like someone who really knows.

Note: Keep meditating on these insights throughout this week and prayerfully apply them to relevant areas of your life and even those of others.

Prayer Focus: Say these prayers for each day as you meditate on the insights received.

Day 1: I declare today that greater is He that is in me than he that is in the world.

Day 2: I command every satanic activity in my life and family to stop now in Jesus' Name.

Day 3: Satan, take your filthy hands off my destiny and finances in Jesus' Name.

Day 4: Arrows of premature death sent against me and family, backfire in Jesus' Name.

Day 5: I cover everyone connected to me in the Blood of Jesus. No more evil news.

Day 6: Father, please never grant the enemies permission to touch me. Shield me daily.

Day 7: Father, I thank You for Your faithfulness to me. Please keep defending me.

Week Forty-Seven

Study Focus: Tell Jesus as It Is
Scriptural Text: Hebrews 4:14-16

Insights for Meditation and Prayerful Application

Hebrews 4:14-16 says "Seeing then that we have a great high priest, that is passed into the heavens, Jesus the Son of God, let us hold fast our profession. For we have not an high priest which cannot be touched with the feeling of our infirmities; but was in all points tempted like as we are, yet without sin. Let us therefore come boldly unto the throne of grace that we may obtain mercy, and find grace to help in time of need."

Once you have surrendered your life to Jesus, you can afford to be very naked with Him. You are free to tell Him exactly how you feel in your body, concerning your job, about your marriage etc. The Lord wants to fix everything that needs to be fixed in your life because He feels what you feel and wants you comfortable. Begin to use your privileges. God bless you mightily.

Note: Keep meditating on these insights throughout this week and prayerfully apply them to relevant areas of your life and even those of others.

Prayer Focus: Say these prayers for each day as you meditate on the insights received.
Day 1: Worship the Lord and tell Him about your spiritual needs.
Day 2: Worship the Lord and tell Him about your family needs.
Day 3: Worship the Lord and tell Him about your emotional needs.

Day 4: Worship the Lord and tell Him about your financial needs.
Day 5: Worship the Lord and tell Him about your health needs.
Day 6: Worship the Lord and tell Him about every other issue bothering you.
Day 7: Give the Lord elaborate thanks for listening to you and for solving your problems.

Week Forty-Eight

Study Focus: Top Secret: Man Can Become a Mountain
Scriptural Text: Psalm 125:1

<u>Insights for Meditation and Prayerful Application</u>
"Those who trust in the Lord are steady as Mount Zion, unmoved by any circumstance"-Psalm 125:1 *(TLB)*

"...his heart is fixed, trusting in the Lord"-Psalm 112:7 *(KJV)*

'Those who trust in the Lord' according to the text above means it is not what everyone does. Trusting in the Lord is a choice. Some may choose to trust in chariots and horses (Psalm 20:7); some may choose to trust in riches (Proverbs11:28, 1Timothy 6:17); some may choose to trust in flesh i.e. men (Jeremiah 17:5); some trust in friends and spouse (Micah 7:5) etc. But for as many as will trust in the LORD, they will be steady; unmoved by any circumstances.

Who then is the LORD? And what does it mean to trust in Him? According to Malachi 3:6, the LORD is the One who changeth not; and according to Psalm 24:8, He is the One who is strong, mighty and mighty in battle. In addition to these, Psalm 24:1 says the Lord is the Owner of the earth and all that is in it. Summarily, the Lord is the Eternal One with all power in heaven and the earth –Psalm 62:11.

Now, to trust in Him means to rely on Him, depend on Him, put confidence in Him and allowing Him to have His way in your life even when you don't understand – Isaiah 50:10. To trust in the Lord is to make boasts in His Name, believing He cannot fail you. One great reason a man should trust in the Lord is the fact that He remains the same throughout eternity – Hebrews 13:8, Malachi 3:6.

Our opening text also describes those who trust in the Lord as Mount Zion which is immovable by any circumstance. Now, a mountain is a fixed entity; it doesn't move. It remains steady and stable year in year out regardless of the climatic condition, economic condition or environmental condition. For instance let 1 million strong men surround a mountain and push with all their energies, the mountain will not move an inch. Let there be thunder, storms, flood etc, the mountain remains steady. During the time of Noah, the rain which destroyed the living things on earth fell for 40 days and 40 nights, covering the whole earth surface for 150 days. Even at that, it only covered the mountains, it didn't move any. It uprooted trees, destroyed houses, floated the ark but didn't uproot the mountains. In fact, the indicator used in confirming that the flood had subsided was that the top of the mountains were seen – Genesis 8:5. This means as terrible as the flood was, while other things perished the mountains survived it. Though they were covered, yet they resurfaced.

Now, when you put your trust in the Lord with a fixed heart, you are like such mountains, unmoved by any circumstance. 'Any' here means no matter what –hunger, thirst, famine, bad news, nakedness, persecutions, disappointment, false accusations, barrenness etc. None of these things moves you- Acts 20:24.

Even when you are trusting in the Lord and it seems as if the floods have covered you, just remain steady, you will surely resurface –no flood can sweep you off. Trust in the Lord. It has never been recorded that a mountain moved because economic policies became unfavorable or because there was a political crisis. Nothing moves it; it abides forever- Psalm 125:1. So, trusting in God makes you unmoved while being moved or concerned is a clear sign of lack of trust in Him.

Note: Keep meditating on these insights throughout this week and prayerfully apply them to relevant areas of your life and even those of others.

Prayer Focus: Say these prayers for each day as you meditate on the insights received.

Day 1: Heavenly Father, please forgive me for putting my trust in wrong places.

Day 2: Father, I put my total trust in You today. Please do not let me fall.

Day 3: Father, please be my Good Shepherd indeed. Uphold me by Your grace.

Day 4: I reject everything contending with my trust in God. I refuse to be moved.

Day 5: Father let me overcome the water of trouble covering me. Make me victorious.

Day 6: The power that floated Noah's ark begins to work in my favor in Jesus' Name.

Day 7: Father, please don't let me be ashamed of my trust and hope in You.

Week Forty-Nine

Study Focus: Please Never Forget This
Scriptural Text: I Corinthians 10:13

<u>**Insights for Meditation and Prayerful Application**</u>
What you are passing through must never paint God as unfaithful. As a matter of fact, it is His faithfulness that will bring you out of the mess you are in. I Corinthians 10:13 says *"There hath no temptation taken you but such as is common to man: but God is faithful, who will not suffer you to be tempted above that ye are able; but will with the temptation also make a way to escape, that ye may be able to bear it."* God is always faithful, please NEVER FORGET THAT!
Shalom!

Note: Keep meditating on these insights throughout this week and prayerfully apply them to relevant areas of your life and even those of others.

Prayer Focus: Say these prayers for each day as you meditate on the insights received.
Day 1: Father, thank You for Your faithfulness over my spiritual life.
Day 2: Father, thank You for Your faithfulness over my family members.
Day 3: Father, thank You for Your faithfulness over my finances.
Day 4: Father, thank You for Your faithfulness over my health.
Day 5: Father, thank You for Your faithfulness over my ministry/career.
Day 6: Father, thank You for keeping me standing despite all the temptations I face.

Day 7: Father, thank You because Your faithfulness will see me through to Heaven.

Week Fifty

Study Focus: Time and Eternity
Scriptural Text: Ecclesiastes 3:1-8

<u>Insights for Meditation and Prayerful Application</u>
In Ecclesiastes 3:1-8 the Bible says '...there is ...a time for every purpose under heaven: a time to be born, and a time to die...' And Hebrews 9:27 says once a man dies, judgment is what follows.
From these, it becomes crystal clear that all events on earth are regulated by time. The moment a man is conceived in his mother's womb, time starts counting. But the moment a man dies, time stops for him and eternity (timeless, unending life) begins.

Now, this eternity has two sides – the **Joyful Eternity** and the **Sorrowful Eternity**. These are otherwise referred to as Heaven and Hell respectively.
The ticket to Heaven is salvation through Jesus Christ (Matthew 1:21; John 3:16-17) while the ticket to Hell is sin (Ezekiel 18:4, 20; Revelation 20:15; 21:8).

Now that you are alive, what can you do?
Firstly, decide where you want to spend your eternity (Heaven or Hell). Then, get the ticket to your chosen eternal destination and keep it safe till you arrive there.
This means you are expected to use your 'time' here on earth to adequately prepare for the eternity (timeless life) that you have chosen. The choice is absolutely yours.
But in case your decision is to arrive in Heaven after leaving this earth,

quickly say this prayer: *Lord Jesus, I am sorry for all my sins. Please forgive me, wash me in Your precious Blood and write my name in the Book of Life. I surrender my life to You from this moment. Help me to spend my eternity in Your Kingdom. Thank You for saving me.*

Congratulations. Please keep your ticket (salvation) safe till you arrive in Heaven (Revelation 3:11). See you there.

Shalom!

Note: Keep meditating on these insights throughout this week and prayerfully apply them to relevant areas of your life and even those of others.

Prayer Focus: Say these prayers for each day as you meditate on the insights received.

Day 1: Father, thank You for the provision of salvation through Your Son Jesus Christ.

Day 2: Powers dragging me and my family to a sorrowful eternity, be destroyed now.

Day 3: Father, release the wisdom to live for You on earth to me in Jesus' Name.

Day 4: Heavenly Father, please change times and seasons in my favor in Jesus' Name.

Day 5: Lord Jesus, at the end of my sojourn here on earth, let me see Your face in glory.

Day 6: I receive grace to be pleasing unto God in every area of my life in Jesus' Name.

Day 7: Father, please let me end my journey in Your joyful kingdom. See me through.

Week Fifty-One

Study Focus: "Musicotherapy"
Scriptural Text: I Samuel 16:14-16

Insights for Meditation and Prayerful Application

In I Samuel 16:14-16, a tormenting spirit came upon King Saul and filled him with depression and fear. On discovering this, his aides suggested a cure. "We will find a good harpist to play for you whenever the tormenting spirit is bothering you; …. The harp music will quiet you and you'll soon be well again". (TLB) verse 23 says "And whenever the tormenting spirit from God troubled Saul, David would play the harp and Saul would feel better; and the evil spirit would go away".

Are you distressed? Are you anxious or nervous? Are you afraid? Are you depressed? Are you confused? Or are you even tired of everything about this life? Don't give up, just get a good music, listen to it and sing along. In fact, you may even take a step further by dancing to the music. Let it be the music that lifts your spirit, not worthless music. Music has a very powerful curative quality for stress, depression and the likes.

Did you remember Elisha in 2 Kings 3:14-15? He got angry and couldn't prophesy again i.e his spirit was troubled with anger thereby making him unable to hear from God.

What was the remedy? He requested that a musical instrument be played, and as soon as there was music, his spirit got back to its healthy state and he started prophesying again. The Bible has recommended 'musicotheraphy' for worries, fears, anxieties, stress, depression etc. Start practicing it and you will be free from them all. Let nothing take away godly music from your life. It heals.

Note: Keep meditating on these insights throughout this week and prayerfully apply them to relevant areas of your life and even those of others.

Prayer Focus: Say these prayers for each day as you meditate on the insights received.

Day 1: Pick a song in Your local dialect and praise the Lord with it today.

Day 2: Get a hymn book and sing thanksgiving hymns to God today.

Day 3: As you go about your activities today, make melodies in your heart to the Lord.

Day 4: Father, please don't allow evil music to be heard in my habitation.

Day 5: Father, please restore all backsliders today in Jesus' Name. Show mercy Lord.

Day 6: Father, please fill my mouth with Your songs of praise.

Day 7: Father, as I sing to You today, please take away my worries, pains and anxieties.

Week Fifty-Two

Study Focus: It Has Been the Hedge
Scriptural Text: Job 1:6-10

Insights for Meditation and Prayerful Application

"Now there was a day when the sons of God came to present themselves before the Lord, and Satan came also among them. And the Lord said unto Satan, Whence comest thou? Then Satan answered the Lord, and said, From going to and fro in the earth, and from walking up and down in it. And the Lord said unto Satan, Hast thou considered my servant Job, that there is none like him in the earth, a perfect and an upright man, one that feareth God, and escheweth evil? Then Satan answered the Lord, and said, Doth Job fear God for nought? Hast not thou made an hedge about him, and about his house, and about all that he hath on every side? thou hast blessed the work of his hands, and his substance is increased in the land." – Job 1:6-10.

You hear about the evil happening around you but none comes to you, you succeed where others fail, you survived what killed others, you enjoy sound health in the midst of sick people, you are financially blessed in the midst of economic hardship etc. These are not as a result of your righteousness, fasting or vigil, neither do they imply that the devil didn't make efforts at destroying you; all you have simply enjoyed is the HEDGE of the Lord. The devil gave us a very important revelation in Job 1:9; he said he couldn't attack Job because of the Hedge the Lord surrounded him with. That is exactly what you are also enjoying. It has been the Hedge. Spend quality time this new week thanking God for His Hedge over your life.

Note: Keep meditating on these insights throughout this week and prayerfully apply them to relevant areas of your life and even those of others.

Prayer Focus: Say these prayers for each day as you meditate on the insights received.

Day 1: Spend some time praising the Lord for His protection over you till this moment.

Day 2: Father, thank You for Your hedge of protection over me and my family.

Day 3: Father, thank You for all the battles You have hitherto fought for me.

Day 4: Father, please let Your hedge over me and my family never be removed.

Day 5: Father, please keep me from offending You. Help me to live holy like You.

Day 6: Father, please silence the devil and all his works in my life and ministry.

Day 7: Father, thank You for all You will do for me and my family in this coming year.

Become a Financial Partner with Jesus

At *Global Emancipation Ministries - Calgary*, our mandate is *to liberate men through the knowledge of the Truth* and our mission statement is *creating channels through which men can encounter the Truth [Isaiah 61:1-3; John 8:32, 36; I Thessalonians 5:24]*.

Our Ministerial Activities include Rural and Urban Evangelical Outreaches, Prison Evangelism, Hospital Ministrations, Mobilization for Missions Support, Teaching of the undiluted Word of God, Scripture-Based Seminars, Discipleship, Training of Field Missionaries and Empowerment of underprivileged ones among other Field Ministerial Tasks.

If you sense the Lord is calling you to reach out to the lost by engaging in any of these activities or by assisting those involved with your resources, please feel free to join us. Let us come together as we take the Gospel of our Lord Jesus Christ to the hurting and forgotten ones. [Mark 16:15-20].

Please join us in these kingdom projects by making your weekly, monthly, quarterly or annual donations to Global Emancipation Ministries – Calgary.

You can visit the "GIVE" section on our website, www.gloem.org, to learn about other ways to give.

For acknowledgement, please advise your donations to us by email: info@gloem.org or emancipation4souls@yahoo.com, and kindly include your details i.e. name, address, email and location. Alternatively, you can simply call +1 587 9735910 to do same.

You can also volunteer your gifts and talents in the service of the Lord through our ministerial platforms regardless of your location. To get information on how to go about this, please visit www.gloem.org and contact us via email: info@gloem.org or emancipation4souls@yahoo.com.
God bless you.

About the Author

By the special grace of God, **Anthony O. Adefarakan** is the privileged President of **Global Emancipation Ministries - Calgary (GLOEM)** with headquarters in Canada, North America and **Emancipating Truth Ministry International (ETMI)** with headquarters in Nigeria, West Africa. The Lord called him into the field ministry in February 2008 with the mandate to liberate men through the knowledge of the Truth, and by December 2012 he was ordained and commissioned as the Pioneer Pastor – in – Charge of The Redeemed Christian Church of God, Revelation Parish, Shalom Area under Delta Province III, Nigeria where he served until 1st February 2015 when he officially handed over to a new Pastor in order to focus on his field ministry to which the Lord had earlier called him and for which the authority of the church had already prayed and released him to undertake.

On 29th September 2013, he was awarded a Post Graduate Diploma in Tent – Making Mission from the Redeemed Christian School of Missions, Nigeria (RECSOM, Asaba Campus) where he also had the privilege to train Pastors and Missionaries as a lecturer in 2017.

Since the commissioning of his field ministry in 2015 he has had the opportunity to lead his ministry officers to field ministrations in different Prisons, Hospitals, Orphanages, Rural communities, Camp settlements, Markets, Local churches among other places with great successes on all occasions – such as salvation of sinners, healing of the sick, financial empowerment of mission churches, provision of relief materials to the poor, provision of medical services to the underprivileged, baptism in the Holy Ghost, deliverance from demonic oppression, release of inmates just to mention a few - all to the glory of God Who alone is the Doer.

He is the author of other best-selling titles such as *Learning from the Ants, It's Your Size, The Immutability of God's Counsel, Surely there is an End, Life Applicable lessons from the Book of Ruth, The Law of Kinds, One thing is Needful , Life Applicable Revelations from God's Word* among others.

He is happily married to Ifeoluwa A. Adefarakan and their marriage is fruitful to the glory of God.

Jesus is his Message, Freedom is the Outcome!
Isaiah 61:1-3

www.ingramcontent.com/pod-product-compliance
Lightning Source LLC
Chambersburg PA
CBHW071851070526
44583CB00016B/1636